ALWAYS
FRESH

ALWAYS FRESH

THE UNTOLD STORY OF

TIM HORTONS

BY THE MAN WHO CREATED

A CANADIAN EMPIRE

RON JOYCE

WITH ROBERT THOMPSON

HarperCollins*PublishersLtd*

Always Fresh
© 2006 by Ron Joyce.
All rights reserved.

Published by HarperCollins Publishers Ltd

Originally published in hardcover by HarperCollins Publishers Ltd: 2006
This trade paperback edition: 2007

HarperCollins books may be purchased for educational, business,
or sales promotional use through our Special Markets Department.

HarperCollins Publishers Ltd
2 Bloor Street East, 20th Floor
Toronto, Ontario, Canada
M4W 1A8

www.harpercollins.ca

Library and Archives Canada Cataloguing in Publication is available

RRD 9 8 7 6 5 4 3 2 1

This book is the author's personal story, and is not published,
authorized or endorsed by Tim Hortons Inc. or any of its affiliates.

Design by Sharon Kish
Printed and bound in the United States

For Amazing Grace

CONTENTS

FOREWORD

It is hard to go anywhere within Canada without seeing a Tim Hortons. They dot the Canadian landscape from St. John's to Victoria. Millions of Canadians head to Tim Hortons to jump start their day each and every morning, regardless of whether it is a hot summer day in July, or deep with snow in February. The chain now employs more than 70,000 Canadians.

In truth, the success of Tim Hortons is, in many ways, a testament to the vision and spirit of Ron Joyce, one of Canada's most legendary and successful businessmen. Even when Ron and his partner Tim Horton had nothing more than a simple store in an area just outside downtown Hamilton, Ron had bigger plans in mind.

Despite a success that has touched almost every Canadian who has been tempted by a Timbit, nothing came easily to Ron. As he clearly demonstrates in Tims, Ron rose beyond a humble upbringing and after serving the public for more than a decade in the Canadian Navy and Hamilton Police Force, he became involved in the food services industry. In 1962, during a time when he was sometimes working three jobs to support his family, the notion that one day he would lead the country's largest restaurant chain seemed laughable. But success was right around the corner—quite literally, as it turned out.

To many who see Tim Hortons restaurants scattered throughout Canada and the Northern U.S., the chain seems almost ubiquitous. The truth is that when Ron started with Tim Hortons it was far from a definite success. In fact, the double-double you drink today from Tims may not have been available without the dogged persistence of Ron. There were many times in the early years of the chain when it might have failed altogether were it not for the hard work and sacrifices Ron, along with the many pioneers who owned the earliest Tim Hortons franchises, were willing to endure.

In many ways Ron's story is more than just the saga of the creation of a restaurant chain. It is the tale of one man's entrepreneurial passion and strong convictions, often under substantial financial strain. Even when the restaurant became a success in Ontario, Ron was not satisfied. Despite the death of his friend and partner, Tim Horton, Ron pushed forward with a strategy to make Tim Hortons the biggest and best food services business in the country. That's not to say it wasn't without its challenges. He competed aggressively with rivals and survived several general economic downturns in the economy. He silenced naysayers who told him the chain would never work outside of Ontario when he successfully launched Tim Hortons in Atlantic and Western Canada.

Beyond business, Ron has also been one of Canada's most benevolent leaders. He used his good fortune at Tim Hortons to help millions of underprivileged children throughout Canada and the United

States. For more than three decades he's been one of Canada's top philanthropists, and his creation of the Tim Hortons Memorial Camp in 1975, followed by the establishment of the Tim Horton Children's Foundation, are indicative of the deep passion he has for helping those less fortunate. As this book documents so well, maybe even more than Tim Hortons, the foundation is Ron's legacy to Canada.

As noted in the documentation, Ron has been honoured many times as a successful businessman and humanitarian. I have had the pleasure of being with Ron at several of these functions and what never ceases to amaze me is the number of individuals and organizations who have benefited from Ron's dedication and commitment. One leaves the room with pride and compassion upon hearing the many tributes directed his way.

Ron loves life and lives it to the fullest. Everything he does, he does with vigour. Some people have dreams. Ron has spent his life chasing and living his dreams from the development of Tim Hortons, to the establishment of the foundation, to his more recent development of his magnificent resort, Fox Harb'r in his beloved native province of Nova Scotia. Perhaps one of his most enduring qualities is that given his renowned success, he is still the very down-to-earth, straight-talking, pragmatic individual everyone has always known.

In the end, a great deal of Ron's success comes down to his ability to focus on tasks and challenges that may seem simple to many. The truth is that his competitors could never rival his strong notions of what Tim Hortons should be and exactly how it should be run. As this book clearly shows, Ron Joyce has set an example for every Canadian who has ever wanted to follow their passion and try their hand in the difficult world of business. As we see repeatedly in the forthcoming pages, there is still room in the world for a good idea, and for people who are willing to work hard to make that idea a success. The truth be told, if our country's future involved the development of more men and women like Ron, Canada's economic future is secure. And more important, if every friend would be the same as Ron Joyce, life would be much more enjoyable.

—The Honourable Ed Lumley

PROLOGUE

To the people who crowded around a brilliant new building on August 2, 1995, the significance of the event must have seemed obvious. On this windy day in Ancaster, Ontario, Tim Hortons, the company I grew from obscurity to become the dominant Canadian restaurant chain, was preparing to open its 1,000th store. It was a major milestone, and the approximately 300 people who attended the grand opening seemed to be aware that they were participating in part of business history.

Thirty years earlier, Tim Hortons had started in Hamilton, only a short drive down the escarpment on the highway from the new restaurant in Ancaster. At that time there was only a single location on Ottawa Street, just outside the city's downtown core. Over the next three decades, it would grow into the country's largest domestic food-service business. Canadians had grown up on Tim Hortons: they had eaten our crullers after dunking them in a steaming double-double; taken home boxes of Timbits for their families; and kick-started their workday by stopping at one of our stores to buy a coffee and a muffin. They identified with the grassroots appeal of the chain and embraced it in a way unlike any other restaurant north of the 49th parallel. In many places in Canada, Tim Hortons was a pub without alcohol. It was a place where people would go to slip away from work, socialize, read newspapers and catch up with their friends. It was a meeting place beloved by millions of Canadians across the country.

Though the company still shared its name with my friend, Tim Horton, it had long since outgrown its link to the late hockey great who helped found it. From its humble beginnings in an old service station, Tim Hortons had come to employ thousands in its stores, warehouses and offices and had become part of Canadian culture. The opening of the 1,000th store demonstrated just how far the business had come from its struggles to keep afloat in its nascent years, when drinking coffee and eating donuts was a foreign concept to many Canadians.

While those in attendance in the mid-afternoon sun awaited the celebration that a corporate milestone typically entails, they were unaware of the true significance of the event. Behind the smiles and handshakes of executives from TDL, the parent company of Tim Hortons, and Wendy's, who were partnering with us to open their 4,500th store, something was brewing that would fundamentally alter one of the greatest businesses ever developed in Canada.

If the facial expressions of any of the executives of Tim Hortons in attendance gave anything away, it would likely have been lost on those who came to shake the hand of Dave Thomas, Wendy's friendly faced founder and pitch man, who had flown in for the ceremony. Thomas, who started Wendy's in 1969, had become a celebrity with a profile that rivalled that of a Hollywood actor, having appeared in hundreds of television commercials for the company.

Thomas had been present in Canada fairly regularly for ribbon cuttings and other events in the four years since the two companies had struck a partnership. This alliance resulted in the creation of so-called "combo stores," which saw Tim Hortons outlets paired with Wendy's restaurants across Canada. The arrangement had been a huge success for Tim Hortons, but Wendy's, which had struggled financially in Canada, had been the true beneficiary of the deal.

By three o'clock that afternoon, with the wind picking up, TDL spokeswoman Patti Jameson introduced the top executives from both companies, including TDL president Paul House and, from Wendy's, CEO Gord Teter, chairman Jim Near and Thomas. The crowd was filled with other local notables, including Hamilton Mayor Bob Morrow and Ancaster Mayor Bob Ward, and fireworks went off as the ribbon-cutting ceremony for the new combo store commenced.

The opening of the new store was the conclusion of a strategy that TDL had developed for Tim Hortons five years earlier. The aim was to double the size of the chain within half a decade. As it happened, the demand for Tim Hortons restaurants across Canada, in towns small and large, in universities and service stations, meant we would eclipse our goal by a wide margin. In 1995 alone, the company opened nearly 300 restaurants. By the end of the year, more than 1,200 Tim Hortons dotted the Canadian landscape, with a few inroads being made into border towns in the U.S.

Following the conclusion of the grand opening, the group of executives from TDL and Wendy's, as well as their invited guests, retreated to the Reimer Corporate Centre, a convention hall located twenty minutes away in Burlington. It was still light outside as people filed into the main room for the reception. During this lull, Gord Teter approached me.

"Ron, let's work through some of the details of the deal," he said. Teter had grown up in the U.S. Midwest, and played football and baseball at Purdue University before obtaining a master's degree in Business Administration. Though many of Wendy's executives were heavy-set, Teter kept himself in good shape, despite being a chain smoker. He was personable man, though he failed to display the same warmth of character that one noticed in Thomas, his charismatic mentor at the burger chain.

"The deal," as Teter put it, had been the focus of our attention at TDL for weeks. Only a handful of people at the reception or the ribbon cutting that afternoon were even aware of any negotiations between TDL and Wendy's. But the truth was, Teter and I were preparing to merge our two companies.

It wasn't the first time TDL had attracted the attention of corporate suitors. At the end of the chain's first decade, Dunkin' Donuts had had the chance to acquire it, but corporate and legal issues quashed a possible transaction. Later, corporate giant Allied Lyons, which controlled one of our flour suppliers, made a pitch to buy TDL. Canadian companies like Scott's Hospitality had also come courting us just as we were expanding our presence across Canada. The most recent suitor had been Cara Operations, the company controlled by the Phelan family. Cara operated several brands, including the Harvey's chain of hamburger restaurants. The company's chairman, Bernie Syron, had spent a fair part of 1995 trying to broker a deal that would have seen Tim Hortons merged with Cara. A deal would have accomplished two things—it would have expanded the Tim Hortons brand in Canada and taken the company onto the public markets. The option of floating an initial public offering of TDL on the Toronto Stock Exchange had even been considered.

But then Wendy's appeared on the scene. In fact, TDL had been partnered with Wendy's on a series of real-estate deals, the basis for the "combo stores" on major roadways, for most of the decade.

For Teter, pulling off the acquisition of TDL and the Tim Hortons brand was integral to his career at Wendy's. The company had stumbled financially heading into the 1990s and its CEO needed to make a deal that would distract investors from the plight of the stores it ran, which were burdened by high costs and the inability to turn a profit. TDL and Tim Hortons, on the other hand, were poised to double in size again in the following five years. From 1991 to 1995, systemwide revenue for TDL had grown from U.S.$308 million to U.S.$541 million. Company profits had risen to U.S.$80 million and growing.

The waiting list for those interested in acquiring a Tim Hortons franchise had thousands of names on it. Those who were lucky enough to open a Tim Hortons store could be assured of double-digit margins and the prospect of paying off their initial investment in a few years. If there was ever a sure thing, owning a Tim Hortons franchise was it. For TDL, the demand for stores and the further expansion of the chain also meant millions to its balance sheet.

I wanted to speak further to Teter about the deal, but the room was becoming too noisy and didn't offer the needed privacy. "Ron, there has got to be somewhere quiet where we can go to talk about this deal," Gord said.

We looked around the main reception room. After some discussion, it was determined, as strange as it sounds, that the men's washroom would provide our best opportunity to sneak away from the crowd. Many of the details of the transaction had already been negotiated by this point, and so, as we spoke, Teter took out a red marker and a piece of paper and, leaning against the wall, began writing down the terms (see page 241). It was the final deal in principle, though some facets were later altered, and it was to close by January 1, 1996. Teter noted my compensation, an estimated 16.2 million shares, adding details about personal jets and the repayment of company loans. A discussion ensued about some real estate in Campbellville, Ontario, which I wanted donated to the Tim Horton Children's Foundation, and the company planes, which I did not want to include in the merger. But largely our bathroom negotiations went smoothly. The major points were marked down, and with a handshake and a signature in red marker, the deal was consummated. When all was said and done, the pact would be worth nearly $600 million. It was an immense amount of money, considering I'd purchased the first restaurant in 1965 for $10,000.

It would take a week for the transaction to be made public. When it was finally announced, it made headlines: "Wendy's puts U.S.$425 million bite on Tim Hortons," blazed one; "Betting dollars on donuts pays off," read another. It was heralded as a great move for me, and by many as providing a great opportunity for a Canadian company.

Far from resting on my laurels, I was already looking to the future. Though some saw it as the end of my time with Tim Hortons, I thought of the sale as giving me the opportunity to become the largest shareholder in a much larger business than TDL. I had two seats on the Wendy's board, which would enable me to influence the direction of the company. From my perspective, it was a merger of two great companies that would revolutionize the food-service industry. It would give TDL a great opportunity to use the American might of Wendy's to bring Tim Hortons to the U.S. with more marketing power than we had ever been able to muster to that point. That was my dream.

Unfortunately, it didn't work out that way.

1

SMALL-TOWN START

To the native band and the French settlers that came to the area, Tatamagouche meant "meeting of the waters." To me, it was the small town where the Waugh and French rivers met, and where I grew up. The Waugh was once one of the great salmon rivers in eastern Canada, though it has diminished with time. Today, Tatamagouche is just another little village that dots the map of Nova Scotia.

The village was built on one of the main trading routes between Prince Edward Island and Halifax, thus giving it a degree of importance during the eighteenth and nineteenth centuries. It had been settled by French Huguenots who fled Europe to avoid persecution, which led to the area being largely Protestant. Many would receive land grants. The Huguenots had largely been labourers—hard-working and with low expectations—and they farmed the land and fished to support themselves. In many ways, that situation hadn't changed in the area by the time I was born in 1930.

By that time, the effects of the Depression were being felt across Canada. It hit Tatamagouche doubly hard, since it was not a part of the country that had been witness to the economic successes Canada had seen in the 1920s. Though industrialization had gone forward in many parts of the country, Tatamagouche was still reliant on farming, lumbering and fishing. With the Depression in full swing, many in the area found themselves unemployed and without any means of making a living. It was a tough, hard world to be born into, and my parents struggled with the economic situation at the time.

My father, Willard, who went by Bill, came from Westville, a small mining town near New Glasgow, near the Northumberland Strait. He was involved in the construction business and met my mother in Tatamagouche in 1929 when he was working on a project to build the Bank of Nova Scotia branch that still stands today. She was just eighteen. They married and I was born a year later, the first of three children.

After their marriage, they moved to Westville, but it was hard to find work in trades as most development in the area had slowed or stopped altogether. Construction projects were few and far between, which made it difficult for my father to land jobs, let alone ones that lasted for any period of time. It is odd, given my young age at the time, but there are two incidents involving my father that I recall vividly. The first is an occasion when he came home one time with three freshly caught salmon. Money was tight, so I don't know if they were caught legally, but I recall quite clearly that Mom was quite upset that he had laid the fish on the kitchen floor for her to clean. Even though it was good to have food in the house, I suspect she was not thrilled with the fish smell throughout her home.

Another time, when I was very young, I entered the barn next to the house. Resting against a beam, there was a hive of honeybees. While trying to get access to the honeycomb, I was stung badly. My father decided the situation had to be resolved before I tried to do it again, so he went in with some friends and used a crowbar to break open the beam where the bees were residing. Once he jostled the beam, the bees became agitated and started swarming. I can recall everyone running and laughing as they tried to escape the angry bees.

The reason I do not remember more about my father is that he wasn't with us long. I was just three when he caught a lift from friends in a pickup truck. He was in the back of the truck, and during the trip a barrel of oil began to tumble out of the vehicle. He tried to stop it from rolling out, but he lost his balance and was carried out of the truck. The barrel landed on him, killing him instantly.

At the age of twenty-three, when she became a widow, my mother had two children and was pregnant with her third. Though my father had a number of brothers and sisters in the area, there was little reason for Mom to stay in Westville. With this in mind, she decided to return to her roots and head back to Tatamagouche, where her parents and siblings lived. This decision didn't make it any easier to come up with money. She received a widow's allowance of $20 per month, so she rented a home on the village's main street at $7 a month. It proved to be more than she could afford, so she determined it would be best to use the life insurance—$1,000 in total—to buy a small house in the village for $500.

The house was tiny, painted white and came with an acre of land. There were three rooms: a main entrance that led into the living room, a small back room where my sister and mother slept, and a small upstairs room that I shared with my brother. There were two beds in the house, both of which were shared. It was simply a bungalow with none of the amenities one might expect, even for the time. There was no running water, no electricity and no insulation to speak of. The house was heated year round by a wood-burning stove in the middle of the living room. It was the only source of heat in the winter, and was also used for all of the cooking and baking. Surprisingly, given its size and age, the little house still exists. Someone purchased the property where it rested a number of years ago and, strangely, decided to move the house across the village. It is now abandoned at the end of a dirt road on the outskirts of Tatamagouche.

Though living without plumbing may seem like desperate circumstances today, it wasn't unheard of in the area at that time. I still recall how cold it was when I had to get up at night during the winter and traipse outside to use the facilities.

Despite my modest upbringing, Tatamagouche provided interesting options for a child. The wharf in town was a busy spot in the summer months and a location where I spent a lot of my early childhood fishing and swimming, as the salt water was quite warm. Though I enjoyed Tatamagouche, the family's tight financial straits forced my mother to send me away to my father's relatives for a number of summers when I was growing up. She was working several jobs, but it was hardly enough to support three children. I was young and didn't understand what was going on, but I did have a sense that I was getting shuffled around a lot. My mother would put me on the train and I would get off in Westville and walk to my grandparents' home.

My grandparents were not young people, and a number of my father's siblings still lived with them at home. My uncle, Tom Joyce, was a successful general contractor, and he employed a lot of his family in that business. They were all hard-working people, doing trades like bricklaying, plastering and carpentry. This left them little time to deal with a young child who had been dropped off for a few weeks at a stretch.

Even as a young boy, I was never happy with my living circumstances. Being part of the welfare system, since my mother was on widow's allowance, meant that I oftentimes wore second-hand clothing. I was self-conscious about my family's situation. For example, the year-end tradition at junior schools in Nova Scotia is to exchange messages and poems in autograph books. I approached my teacher, Mrs. Bell, about having her write in my book. Perhaps I was a bit of a rambunctious child, but what she wrote in the book surprised me:

> *Rich boys have many faults, poor boys have but two:*
> *Nothing is any good they say and nothing is any good they do.*

I remember how much her inscription hurt me at the time. I recall wondering why she had decided to choose that passage. It has stuck with me all of my life. I was never happy being poor, and having it pointed out to me was hurtful.

When I wasn't spending time with my father's parents, I was often at my grandparents on my mother's side, Arch and Minnie Jollymore. One of their neighbours was the only village doctor, Dr. Dan Murray, the grandfather of Canadian singing star Anne Murray.

When I was eight, Canada announced it would enter World War II in support of Great Britain, an event that changed the course of many lives. I still recall our neighbour next door, a relative named Etta Reid, called over to my mother to tell her the news.

"Grace," she said, speaking to my mother, "Great Britain has declared war on Germany!"

Almost immediately my mother began to cry. Given my age, I couldn't understand why the news had such a big impact on Mom. "Declared war" was a phrase that really didn't have any meaning to me.

"Why are you crying, Mom?"

"Well, Ron, Great Britain has declared war on Germany, and that means Canada will be sending men to fight," she explained, sobbing quietly. "A lot of men from Tatamagouche will have to go over, and a lot of them will die."

She was right. Within weeks, many of the young men from the area had departed to join the Canadian Armed Forces. The workforce that manned the local farms, lumber mills and creameries disappeared. It would turn out to be a pivotal point in my young life.

By the time the war had been under way for a couple of years, I was working for my mother's brother, Stan Jollymore, on his farm. There simply was no one else to help him. Managing the farm proved to be a big operation that started at 5 a.m. The cows had to be milked twice a day, and hay and wood had to be cut and harvested. My uncle rarely ever had a day off, but that was the life to which he had grown accustomed.

I grew to like working because it gave me some spending money. I was an average student, strong in math and history, but weak in English grammar. I decided that my future would not involve academics and thought that going to school was simply a waste of time. With the end of the war approaching, I decided that I no longer wanted to attend school; rather, I'd try my luck working full time. I was fifteen and had finished Grade 9. Mom tried everything she could to encourage me to stay in school, but I was very headstrong and I wanted to leave, even though it broke her heart.

Around that time, I had my first major crush, on a girl named Carol Wood. She was beautiful and we would walk to school holding hands.

Though we were close friends, it was clear that she was bound for university, while I was headed somewhere else. She kept telling me I could do more with my life if I stayed in school.

"If you drop out, Ronnie, you'll end up digging ditches," she told me more than once. We split up after I dropped out of school to find work. The first job I found was with a company called Latimer Construction, a business that was paving a road through the village. The company used a number of local teenagers, especially since labour was in short supply. One day I was digging a drainage trench alongside the roadway. As I was working, Carol passed by on her way to school. She looked down at me and said, "I told you so," as she walked away.

However, there wasn't any work in Tatamagouche, so I did what comes naturally to those who are young and need money: I left town. I went in search of seasonal work in the Annapolis Valley, finding a job at a canning factory. The rate of pay was twenty-eight cents an hour and the shifts lasted thirteen hours. It was a taxing job. We would start the day at 6 p.m. and work six nights per week. Of course, since it was seasonal work, once the fruit was all processed, I was given my paycheque and told without notice that my services were no longer needed at the end of the season. The plant simply shut down.

By November 1945 I found myself back at my mother's house and working at the creamery in Tatamagouche, located near the railway station, just off the main street. I paid room and board and was determined to save enough money to go to Ontario. After the war, with all of the men and women returning, there was very little work in Atlantic Canada. The situation triggered a huge migration of people to other parts of Canada, but mainly Ontario, and that's where I decided to go to try to make my way in the world. At the age of sixteen, I realized my future would not be in Tatamagouche. Mom wasn't overly upset about my decision. It was clear that there was not going to be regular work for me in Nova Scotia, and my leaving left her with one less mouth to feed.

My mother has never been pleased with the fact that I've said publicly that we grew up poor. She is a proud person and did the best she could to raise us, given her limited means. I don't think she ever considered herself poor. Though we didn't have much money, I've always admired this marvellous woman who gave up so much to keep us together despite so many difficulties early in her life. Shortly after I left Nova Scotia, she married her long-time friend, Vic Annis, a relationship that would last fifty years until his death in 1997. She has remained in eastern Canada for the rest of her life.

With $35 to my name, I chose to spend most of it on a ticket to Ontario. I had no idea what was in store for me there.

2

STARTING OVER IN STEELTOWN

The decision to leave Nova Scotia was followed by an equally difficult question: Where to go?

I'm not sure exactly why I settled on Hamilton, Ontario. I'd heard that, following the conclusion of the Second World War, the city was very much the centre of Canadian industry. With that in mind, I purchased a $30 train ticket and boarded the train with a bag of belongings and $5 to my name.

The remaining money didn't last very long. Soon after the trip started, I fell in with a group of guys from Cape Breton who seemed determined to have a good time all the way to Ontario. They were playing guitars and fiddles and having the occasional drink to pass the time. This was a welcome distraction as the train, which was an old coal-burning steam engine, had to stop frequently to take on coal and water. When the train stopped in Edmundston, New Brunswick, for fuel, some of the guys took up a collection to buy some beer and sandwiches during the stop. I threw my last five dollars in the hat, but the beer sure tasted great. This meant I got off the train in Hamilton without a dime to my name, in a city that I had never seen before. It was exhilarating. The lights of the city were unlike anything I'd been witness to.

I started walking south on James Street, away from the rail station, and was overwhelmed by how vibrant Hamilton seemed. I'd never been in a city; I was flabbergasted by just how big it appeared, even though Hamilton wasn't that large at the time. It seemed a world away from the small village life of Tatamagouche.

I followed James Street to Cannon, looking for a boarding house that might take me in. I figured I would have to convince someone that my situation warranted special consideration in order to get them to take a chance on me, since I had no money. At 45 Cannon Street West I saw a sign that said, "Boarders wanted." I knocked on the door and it was answered by Mrs. Routley, an older English lady with grey hair and big jowls.

I immediately gave her my best pitch.

"Excuse me, ma'am, but I'm looking for a place to stay. I don't have any money to pay—for now, but I'll get a job and get some money and then I'll be able to pay the room and board."

She stood there for a moment, sizing me up. Then she shook her jowls and answered.

"Okay, you can stay for three days," she said. "But only three days. If you don't have a job by then, you will be out on the street." Despite her gruff demeanour, Mrs. Routley was a kind, gentle person.

She took me up to a tiny room that had four cots in it. I would share the room with three others, and pay her $8.50 per week, which included two meals and a packed lunch. I still didn't have any money, but one of the other boarders gave me a couple of streetcar tickets, which allowed me to start my job search.

It didn't take long to land a job, and in this case it was one that paid big money.

Hamilton at that time was considered a lunch-bucket town, and factories would spring up just as others would close. The city's industrial sector had really expanded during the war, and in the following years, Hamilton's industry continued to grow, though labour tensions often affected companies like Stelco, Westinghouse and Firestone. To meet demand for jobs at these facilities, people like me—from all over Canada—and immigrants from overseas began to converge on the city.

It was into this atmosphere of rapid change that I went looking for a job. On the morning of my second day in Hamilton, I inquired at the American Can Company; I went into their employment office and it turned out they were looking for workers. I didn't have to show them any documents, a resumé or any references. They hired me on the spot.

"When can you come to work?" the gentleman in the office asked.

"As soon as you need me."

"Well, how about three this afternoon?"

I told him that I'd be there and asked how much I would be paid. He said eighty-five cents an hour, which was a big leap from what I'd been making in Nova Scotia.

My role at the plant was simple: I was a stripper, though not in the way the word is used now. I worked in the lithography department, where they took sheets of metal and added print and colour to them before turning them into cans. In some cases the cans had three colours. We would take the sheets, apply the colours, and then send them through the ovens. After they passed through the ovens, the sheets would be stripped and sent on for a second pass, or colouring. My job was to do the stripping. It was a hot, dirty, nasty job, but it paid more money than I had ever earned before.

The only problem was the job was not consistent. Like a lot of positions at companies during the late 1940s, American Can would run out of work and lay off employees without notice. By the fall, I had been laid off twice, so I went in search of other, more reliable, although seasonal, work. I found it in the tobacco fields of southern Ontario, where the money was substantial—up to $25 per day, including room and board.

I worked at several places before settling into a job at the Firestone Tire and Rubber Company on Burlington Street in Hamilton's east end in 1948. I was willing to work double shifts—sixteen hours at a stretch—something that was often frowned upon by some union members, and of course the shop stewards. But my loyalties weren't to the union—and I felt that it was my decision if I was willing to work longer hours. I also agreed to come in on weekends to help clean up. I recall quite specifically that I once made $250 over a two-week stretch, which was more money than I could even conceive of at the time. Though I had worked extraordinarily long hours for the paycheque, I was still thrilled to have access to so much money.

After a year in Hamilton, I decided to go home to see my mother, my brother Willard, known as Bill, and my sister Gwen. But once I returned to the small village that I grew up in, it felt strange. The places I had thought were big and vibrant in Tatamagouche couldn't hold a candle to what Hamilton had to offer. I realized quickly that I could never really live there again. A city, even one like Hamilton that wasn't so large, just offered so much more. Coming to that realization cured me of my homesickness.

Shortly after arriving at the Firestone plant, I had met a lady named

Lynda—a wonderful woman with a big smile who just happened to work two floors below me. Lynda and I were married on my birthday in 1949. We were both nineteen years old.

Two years later, I made a significant decision: I would join the Canadian Navy. I guess I was smitten by the sense of glamour associated with the armed forces, along with the naïveté of youth. I had missed the Second World War because I'd been too young to serve, and in a way I think that joining the navy was a means of trying to experience what so many of my peers had gone through. And, I wanted to see the world. Given that, the navy seemed like a good fit.

Despite my expectations, I didn't actually set sail for almost two years. Before I would be placed on a ship, I had to take basic and communications training, which lasted almost two years at Cornwallis, the basic-training facility for the Canadian Navy near Digby, Nova Scotia. My first tour on a ship, in this case on an aircraft carrier named the HMCS *Magnificent,* commenced in 1953.

I was trained as a wireless operator, and although it seems antiquated today, this was well before satellites made it easy to communicate between seafaring vessels. I had been trained to read and write Morse code, which was the primary form of long-distance communication at sea during the period.

It turned out to be a remarkable experience; the ship toured as part of the coronation of Queen Elizabeth II, and those of us who made up the ship's crew were fortunate to attend the Spithead Review, the largest gathering of international ships ever in peacetime. It was a spectacle I would never forget.

We returned from that trip to Halifax, where I was drafted to HMCS *Iroquois,* a Tribal class destroyer, bound for Korea. The trip had an amazing itinerary, which led us through the Panama Canal and back through the Suez Canal. Along the way, we saw places I never dreamed I would visit.

Though I was determined to gain some of the experience of combat, by the time we arrived in Korea the peace treaty had been signed. That meant the ship was used for peacekeeping duties, providing supplies to smaller South Korean vessels as well as regular patrols. The odd time we would be called to Action Station when Soviet MiGs would violate our air space and play a cat-and-mouse game with U.S. aircraft before returning north of the 38th parallel.

When we left Korea, it was determined that our ship should make a goodwill visit to other countries in the Commonwealth. We visited places like Hong Kong, which was filled at the time with refugees fleeing the communists in mainland China, as well as Singapore, Ceylon, India and Pakistan. Though there was work to be done, there was plenty of time to go ashore and see parts of the countries where we were docked. The hospitality in some places was amazing. Bombay was particularly fascinating—I recall seeing *Gone with the Wind* for the first time there—but the quality of life in that part of the world was very different from what I had become used to back in Hamilton.

We also travelled to India and Pakistan during the time when the two countries were being partitioned, and I witnessed first-hand the amazing influx of refugees between the two countries. Due to the tremendous number of refugees in Karachi, Pakistan, the country was busy building makeshift homes. They would simply take two long concrete-block walls that were divided by further concrete partitions approximately every twenty feet. This space would become shelter for the refugees, who then had to build roofs to protect themselves from the elements. The poverty was occasionally overwhelming. But the trip provided an opportunity to see a wide variety of exotic and interesting cultures, from Aden in eastern Africa, through the Suez Canal, to Cairo. We spent one week in Malta before arriving in Gibraltar for another week. We then stopped in the Azores for refuelling then home to Halifax.

After my navy trip in 1954–55, I dreamed of going on another world tour. The first trip, on a warship, included 250 other men. There was no air conditioning and we slept in hammocks. I could only hope that my second trip, whenever it took place, would be far more comfortable.

ooooo

By 1956, my five-year tour in the navy was nearing completion, and I realized I would have to find something else to do. Though I often returned to Hamilton on leave, which was thirty days per year, by the time I returned to the city permanently after my stint in the Navy, my family life had changed. We now had two children: Gary, born in 1951, and Ron Jr., in 1955.

While I was in the navy, we lived in the naval married quarters. Lynda had to bear the brunt of raising the boys. Upon leaving the navy, I was given a few months to find another job, so I set my sights on becoming a police officer. I had considered law-enforcement work prior to joining the navy, and had even gone as far as to apply for a position. I had always considered police work to be very interesting, perhaps because the local RCMP constable in Tatamagouche was held in very high regard and was a significant part of the community. I aspired to such a status, and I was taken on by the Hamilton police force within weeks of leaving the navy.

Shortly after I joined the police department, we were surprised by the arrival of our twin boys, Derrick and Darrell. Throughout her pregnancy, we had no idea that Lynda was carrying twins.

During my nine years as a member of the Hamilton Police Department, there were many incidents that left me with great memories. I'll recall a few of them. While on patrol with Colin Millar (who would later become Chief Constable of the Hamilton Police Department) we received a call from the dispatcher and were told to check if an ambulance was needed at an apartment building near the Hamilton General Hospital. Once we arrived at the building, I dropped Colin off at the apartment and proceeded to find a place to park.

When I came into the second-floor apartment, Colin pointed to the living room.

"See what you can do in there while I call the hospital," he said, gesturing towards the living room in the apartment. There on the chesterfield was a woman in the advanced stages of childbirth. Her husband and another lady stood nearby, helplessly in shock, not knowing what to do. In those days, police officers received no first-aid training, and even though I was the proud father of four sons, I had never witnessed childbirth. On delivery, the baby girl was not breathing and the umbilical cord was wrapped around her neck. I asked the woman who was in the room to help remove the cord. Finally, with a smack to the baby's bottom, she coughed and started to cry. That sound was a great thrill for all of us to hear.

Colin was still on the phone with the hospital and advised me not to cut the cord, but rather tie it in the middle. I tied it off with my shoelace.

Many years later, Colin's wife Barbara met the young lady we delivered, who was working in a pharmacy in Hamilton. She didn't mention it to Colin until his retirement party as Chief Constable of the Hamilton Police Department, when the young woman was invited as a surprise guest. This whole episode was a wonderful experience.

I can remember another incident on a Sunday night when I was in the east end, driving a motorcycle. There was an all-car call over the radio, with a licence-plate number and a warning that the individuals in several cars were leaving the Burlington area. We were told they were armed and dangerous and to approach with extreme caution. I was on Barton Street, and I saw a car going west that fit the description. Turned out the licence plate was also a match, so I called the dispatcher and requested backup.

There was only one occupant inside the car, so I decided to pull him over. I stopped behind his vehicle and ordered him out of the car. I told him to place his hands flat on the roof—a procedure used then to protect yourself. I had my Smith & Wesson .38 drawn, and about that time my backup arrived. The suspect indicated to them that they should take the weapon from me before I shot somebody. I can only assume my hands were shaking severely.

On another occasion, a high-speed chase started in the west end. Suspects broke into a TV store and scooped several expensive items. It was about 2:00 a.m. and a lot of units were in for lunch, so very little backup was available for Officer Denny Williams, who was alone in his police car. The chase went through the downtown core, up and down one-way streets in the wrong direction. As more police scrambled out to help, I decided to move up to Main Street, which was a four-lane street that ran one way eastbound. I was on my Harley, and I could see them coming at high speed, lights flashing towards me. I headed west, my lights on, ready to get the hell out of the way if they kept coming. They slowed down and turned south on a short street; I was right behind them when they went through a "T" intersection and came to rest up against a tree. By this time there were a lot of police involved, and the suspects leaped out of their cars and scattered.

"If you don't stop, I'll shoot!" I yelled at one of them. I guess he didn't believe me, because he kept running, eventually trying to jump the fence at the end of the alley. While making his escape, he caught the back of his pants on the fence and fell over the other side. The fence was simply too high, so I didn't even bother to try to climb it. Instead, I leaned over it and pointed my gun at him as he lay prone on the ground.

"Stop right there! You're under arrest!" I yelled at him.

But he got up and just started running again, which proved my authority left much to be desired.

As I proceeded back up the alley towards the other side of the building, one of the other suspects ran directly towards me. I grabbed him and handcuffed him to the car door. We had now arrested two of the three culprits. As it turned out, the suspect I had chased over the fence was the owner of the car that was involved in the break-in. Several hours later, he called the police and reported that his vehicle had been stolen. The dispatcher called me to the central station to identify him. Of course, he was easy to identify, but he still maintained that his car had been stolen. I then asked him to stand up and turn around. His pants were ripped where he had jumped the picket fence.

Strangely, the three suspects chose trial by judge and jury. On the first day of the trial before well-known Judge Latchford, the defence lawyer for one of the accused appeared in court in an advanced state of intoxication. Each of the three had quite a criminal track record, but they'd always seemed to get off. This time they were all convicted and served time in prison.

One of the real issues I had with working for the police was the pay. When I finally left the police department, as a first class constable, our annual compensation was less than $5,000, less deductions. This became a problem after my marriage fell apart in 1958. We had faced a lot of difficulties after my return from the navy. Our interests were very different, an issue that became more apparent as time went on. Once our marriage ended, most of my salary went to support Lynda and our four sons. During much of this time I lived in a room that I rented for $12 per week. Even then, with most of my money going to Lynda and the kids, making ends meet was extremely difficult. I would have to find a way to support myself. Thankfully, I had never been afraid of hard work, because that's what it took to keep afloat during those years.

I worked all sorts of second jobs to supplement my income. I drove a produce truck, did construction, was a Brink's guard and served in the Naval Reserve for eight years. All of these jobs brought in money, but didn't get me much further ahead. You weren't supposed to be moonlighting; the police force really frowned upon this. But I didn't have any choice. Although I was never reprimanded, I'm sure they knew what I was doing.

I was now thirty-three years old, working twenty-hour days and still not getting any further ahead. I knew things had to change, and I kept my eyes open for any opportunity that might present itself. Thankfully for me, it wouldn't be long before my fortunes would improve.

3

FROM ICE CREAM TO DONUTS

In 1960, I met and fell in love with Theresa McEwan. Teri, as she preferred to be called, was separated from her husband, Richard. They had two children, Donald and Richard. Our friendship would include many weekends spent with our six boys, and they became a significant part of our relationship. In time, divorces from our respective previous marriages were finalized and we were married in 1963. We both had full- *and* part-time jobs, and we eventually managed to accumulate enough capital to put a small down payment on a triplex on Kensington Avenue North in Hamilton in early 1962. We were struggling, but slowly making headway.

By 1962, I had determined that there must be a better way than putting in long hours at menial second jobs that, while they helped pay my bills, didn't allow me to do much more. I knew two brothers who worked for the Ford Motor Company in Oakville and owned a successful hamburger restaurant called Millionaire at the corner of

Upper James and Mohawk. This was long before franchise systems such as McDonald's, Burger King and Wendy's had broken into the Canadian market.

Not only were the brothers successful, but they were having fun managing their restaurant. While I worked to survive, these guys were having the time of their lives *and* making money doing it. It seemed to me that the food-service industry might provide the break I had been looking for. Unfortunately, I had no idea how to start my own restaurant.

One fall evening when we lived on Kensington Avenue, Teri and I went for a walk that would change our lives forever. We headed four blocks east to the Dairy Queen at London and Main (the store is still operating in the same location today). In the summer, when I would head back and forth from work, I used to see customers standing in long lines for ice cream; but as soon as the weather got cold, the demand disappeared. Not surprisingly, on this particular evening, the shop seemed deserted as we approached.

When we went up to the window, I realized we were being served by George Otterman and his wife, Nancy. George had been a shipmate from the navy days and we had great memories to share. Since there were so few customers, he just closed the shop for the night and invited us in for a drink. We were fascinated by how George and Nancy, who both held full-time jobs, had managed to get into the food business. Before long, we began talking about his experiences managing the Dairy Queen.

"You've got to get yourself one of these, Ron," he said. "They're a licence to print money."

We had a couple more drinks and talked late into the evening. The idea of entering into the food business, which had once seemed so distant, suddenly didn't seem unattainable. In fact, we were very excited with the idea. Once home, I grabbed our copy of the *Hamilton Spectator*. We turned to the "Businesses for Sale" section of the classified ads and, right there in small print, we found what we were looking for: three Dairy Queen franchises for sale. All it took to acquire one was a $200 deposit on an overall payment of $8,000. Thankfully, no payments were required until the store re-opened for the season the following March. For your money you received the lease and all the equipment, as well as three days' training. The arrangement with Dairy Queen meant that you did not pay a royalty to head office, an unusual practice at the time, but you had to buy the ice cream mix and products from them. They had an exclusive formula for their mixes, which they sold at a healthy mark-up in lieu of the royalties.

Our Dairy Queen, which opened in March 1963, turned out to be the best thing that had happened to us financially to that point in our lives. The store performed exactly as we'd been promised. In the first full year we owned it, we managed to make $15,000 in profit—three times the salary I was making as a police officer.

The other aspect of the business that I enjoyed was that we were selling a product that people lined up for—and it was a treat. It was a 180-degree change from my usual "products," like speeding tickets, that usually resulted in very unhappy customers.

It was a seasonal business, which meant that when the weather warmed up the lineups grew longer. Sometimes, the days seemed endless, since I was still working full-time at the police department. However, it could be demoralizing early in the spring when we were preparing for customers and it was still snowing. On a number of occasions, with some solid support from a couple of hired employees, we would sell more than $1,000 worth of ice cream in a single day. That may not sound like a great deal in today's terms, but it translated into hundreds of customers.

One of the things Dairy Queen taught me was the effective use of space. Their stores were very compact; the outlet I owned was only about 700 square feet. That kept walking to a minimum, which boosted efficiency. With little wasted effort, staff could fill the ice cream orders and be immediately ready to take the customer's cash. The proximity of the cash register and products were central to the way I would develop Tim Hortons stores.

The outside of the store provided little protection from the elements, but when the weather was warm, people would show up even when it was raining. Dairy Queen was a pioneer in the food-service business in Canada, which consisted largely of "mom and pop" independent shops. Franchises or chain stores were rare at the time. Over the years, there have occasionally been reports of scams connected with dishonest franchisors, but I think the arrangement with Dairy Queen was very fair. They operated a solid chain. But not everyone was of the same opinion.

About a year after I bought the franchise, a number of disgruntled Dairy Queen owners, led by some operators from Windsor, were forming an association to oppose some of the decisions being made at the company's headquarters. It reminded me of a union meeting. I didn't care for the dictatorial terms of unions when I was an employee; I felt I should be able to determine what was in my best interests. The tone of the meeting was very heated, with the franchisees claiming they were being ripped off by Dairy Queen. While they painted head office as the villains, I felt the franchisees were the ones making ridiculous demands and I told them so.

"I don't want any part of this nonsense," I told them at the meeting. "Though I've only been involved in this for a year or two, I think Dairy Queen has been fair. If we play our part, we'll all do well."

Those comments were not well received, to say the least, but since there was nothing left for me to say, I simply left the meeting. I didn't want any part of their association; I had my store and my job at the police department to worry about. In the end, the association didn't amount to much. Little did I know that, in a few years, I would face a similar problem, but with a twist: I would be the corporate entity that a group of franchise owners would form an association to challenge.

After I spent a year in the business and saw the potential, I became determined to acquire a second franchise. Gary Thompson, the company representative for Dairy Queen, approached me about purchasing a store he was currently building in Oakville on Lakeshore Road. It sounded perfect, except for one thing—we didn't have enough money to acquire it. I tried the traditional route, through the local banks, but they were still concerned about the viability of the outlet we already owned, so they refused to lend us any capital. Running out of options, I went to the Industrial Development Bank, which was a federal institution set up to help people who couldn't get money through more traditional channels. They approved us, based on our success with the first store.

With that, I submitted an application to Dairy Queen head office to acquire the second franchise. It didn't appear that there would be any problems, since I now had access to the capital and a good track record with the first store.

But head office turned us down, saying that we were undercapitalized. Needless to say, I was disappointed because it was a great location. Subsequently, I heard there were problems between Harold Rayme, the president of Dairy Queen of Canada, and Gary Thompson, the site developer. The odd thing about the location was that it became a Country Style donut store that eventually went bankrupt.

ooooo

Following that rejection, I started to investigate other options.

On Ottawa Street, just a short walk from where I lived, sat a converted service station that now housed a store that had only been open for a few months. I had never set foot inside it, but I was aware it was trying to crack an area of the food business that had largely been untouched to that point: the coffee and donut market. It was called Tim Horton's Do-nuts, and since I was having no luck convincing Dairy Queen to sell me another store, I decided to inquire about franchise possibilities with this new restaurant. There was a "Franchise for Sale" sign in the window with a Toronto phone number. I knew little about the donut and coffee business, but I had become obsessed with owning another food-service franchise. I called the number and spoke to a man named Jim Charade. He told me he was a Toronto businessman who had been working with Tim Horton, the defenceman with the Toronto Maple Leafs, for a number of years. I later learned that Charade and Horton had first met in the early 1960s, and Tim had lent his name to a series of hamburger restaurants Charade operated. Eventually, this licensing deal gave way to a partnership, and they ultimately launched the first Tim Hortons* store in Hamilton.

During our first meeting, Jim outlined the store's revenue projections on a paper napkin. The figures impressed me. He said the business was grossing $1,000 per week, with profit margins of between 18

* Initially Tim Hortons used an apostrophe in the name. For consistency, the name "Tim Hortons" is used throughout this book.

and 20 percent. My take from the store would be $200 per week, and since I was making less than $100 a week as a police officer, it would double my annual income. To top it all off, I still had the Dairy Queen, which, though seasonal, continued to be very successful during the warm months.

Charade was a charismatic man, and was able to close deals, which I later found out was the only reason he'd managed to keep their floundering upstart business afloat. The hamburger restaurants opened with Tim Horton in Toronto had been problematic from the start. Dirty and poorly managed, they weren't the kind of places that attracted return customers. It wasn't long before the hamburger restaurants ran into financial turmoil, forcing Jim to shuffle money around to keep them operating.

During this time, Tim went on a cruise with his wife Lori. He was entirely unaware of how precarious the restaurants' finances had become. Meanwhile, Jim took advantage of the Hortons' absence to take what little money remained and plough it into a donut shop on Kingston Road in Toronto, owned by Dennis Griggs, which was having operational problems. By 1964, he would shift his focus to Hamilton.

As it turned out, the Ottawa Street Tim Hortons location had also had a checkered history. There had been two franchise owners in the previous six months—I would later learn that the first owner, Spencer Brown, had had a falling out with Charade and managed to sell his stake in the restaurant at a profit. Additionally, coffee and donut shops were a relativity untested concept at the time. Yet these factors didn't succeed in frightening me off. Perhaps Charade's financial projections, combined with my eagerness and enthusiasm, blinded me to what Jim really had to offer, but I wasn't in a frame of mind to consider the hurdles the business could potentially face. My lawyer at the time, R.T.

(Buck) Bennett, who later went on to became a judge, told me I was crazy to get involved in the deal.

"This isn't like buying the Dairy Queen where you know exactly what you're getting," Buck told me. "Charade doesn't really have anything to sell you."

Buck tried to talk me out of it, but I had made up my mind—I was buying the franchise, even though I had never met the man after whom the store was named.

4

HUMBLE BEGINNINGS

Once I'd committed to the Tim Hortons venture, I decided it was time to leave my job as a police officer. To make the move official, I went to the chief, Leonard Lawrence, and told him that, as much as I enjoyed being on the force, it was time for me to move on and pursue an opportunity in the donut business. He listened to my story and took the letter of resignation I offered him.

"I'm going to take this and put it in my desk," he said. "I'm going to hang onto it, and if you change your mind or if something happens, I'll just tear it up." It was a very kind and fair offer. I'm sure he expected to see me again in a few weeks, but I was determined not to let that happen.

To that end, I borrowed $10,000 from the Hamilton Municipal Credit Union to buy the franchise. The sale price included the store and all of its equipment, furnishings and signage. As part of the arrangement, I would pay Jim Charade and Tim Horton a 2 percent

royalty on gross sales, while also agreeing to purchase all of my supplies from them at a significant mark-up, which was standard in most
franchises at the time. I was also required to pay 2 percent of sales as
an advertising fee, although the company offered no promotional support to speak of.

I started at the restaurant in February 1965. The agreement called
for me to be trained by John Gowan, a Scot who had been managing
the restaurant, and the head baker, Jeff. The pair were both openly gay
and were involved in a relationship. Though I wasn't aware of it at the
time, the relationship between the two men meant they collaborated
on everything involving the restaurant. I was stunned by the way they
went about the baking process. There were no notes, manuals or recipes. Years later, Spencer Brown, the original owner of the franchise,
gave me the manual, such as it was, that he had received to run the
restaurant. Marked "In Strict Confidence," the book is four pages long
and provides vague details on how to make white cake, chocolate and
yeast-raised donuts. Jim Charade never gave me a manual, but even if
he had, I'm sure it wouldn't have been of much help.

Tim Hortons claimed to offer "50 varieties" of donuts, but they
broke down into four basic types: a yeast-raised product, a white cake
donut, a chocolate cake donut, and a French cruller. These would then
be finished with different coatings or fillings to make all of the variations offered for sale in the store.

That seemed reasonable enough, but one thing about the operation
defied all logic: Jeff kicked off the night's baking by taking out a Ouija
board, setting it up and asking it questions. "Ouija board, how many
pounds of flour should I prepare tonight?"

Once the Ouija board's opinion had been divined, Gowan came
back to me.

"So, here's what we're going to do," he said. "We're going to make thirty pounds of yeast, and ten pounds of white cake and ten pounds of chocolate cake," he said. Preparing the donuts was a significant undertaking. Not only did we do all the baking, but we did all the finishing—I thought the whole situation was crazy, but I'd invested money and decided that I'd wait to see how it worked out. Not surprisingly, things didn't immediately improve.

Before long, Gowan showed me what he referred to as "keeper boxes." These were trays of donuts covered in plastic to keep them moist, so overproduction could be used on later days when the store might run short. I also noticed that the store wasn't particularly clean. It had been built in an old service station, so the space was far from ideal for a restaurant, even one that was only serving donuts and coffee. There were no tables, just eleven stools where people could sit and eat their purchase. One wall was plastered with lava rock, and employees would constantly be cutting themselves as they brushed up against it. The entire store was quite small, perhaps 1,200 square feet, and box-like. Customers would enter through the front door into a small vestibule where both washrooms were located. The donut display and a single cash register were located on the left. There was a small counter space where product was sold as take-out, which accounted for 75 percent of our orders. And at the far end of the store was the baking room, which had a window that allowed people to peer in and watch the production. The donuts were finished in a small area just outside the baking room.

The store was open around the clock. During our baking hours, which started in the middle of the night, there would be one person producing the donuts, while the counter would be staffed by a single employee. The morning rush, which was by far the busiest time of day, required us to have three people to serve the customers on their way to work. But by 11 a.m., that rush would be over and the store was again staffed by only one person.

Penny Spicer, who worked steady nights, had been employed at the store under both previous owners. She was very diligent, and she essentially ran the place while Gowan and Jeff produced and finished the donuts in the back.

On one occasion early on, I told Penny the washrooms needed to be cleaned. She looked appalled.

"Mr. Joyce," she said with a disdainful tone in her voice, "I don't clean the washrooms."

With that, I grabbed the mop and cleaning supplies and went and cleaned them myself. I think that demonstrated to her the commitment I had made to the business and won her over. I never had to ask her to clean the bathrooms again—she just did it.

After a few nights of this craziness involving the Ouija board, I'd become pretty dejected. One night, I was sitting in the back, sucking on an orange while I got ready to bake, when Gowan came in.

"Mr. Joyce, don't you ever eat an orange in the baking area. You can contaminate the product," he said in his thick Scottish brogue. That was news to me, so I took the orange and threw it in the garbage.

The next day I was working late after Gowan and Jeff had left, and Penny phoned me.

"Mr. Joyce, I can't stand this anymore," she said. "Mr. Gowan is making a fool of you. He's laughing behind your back and teaching you garbage. That stunt with the orange was just an example of what he's trying to pull."

I was stunned. Why would my instructor, a man who worked for Tim Horton, an NHL hockey star, want to mislead me?

"They don't want you to be successful," she said. "They are setting you up to fail so they can take back the store to manage."

I was horrified. I'd been sold a bill of goods and now I had to figure out how I would fix it. My lawyer, Buck Bennett, had been right: Jim and Tim had no business selling a franchise, especially one with no track record and without a single successful operation anywhere. They really had nothing to sell. But I'd managed to get so pumped up that I had been willing to ignore all the warning signs that were right there in front of me. It took a while for that feeling to wear off and for me to become aware of all the trouble we faced. I had quit my job and borrowed money, and there wasn't any substance to the business that I had purchased.

5

PARTNERS

After the conversation with Penny, I called Jim and informed him what I had learned and indicated that we had to resolve the many problems we were experiencing with the store.

"I want to see you down at the store right away," I continued. "I want some answers."

I firmly told Gowan and his friend to leave my store, but the situation didn't improve with their absence. I was starting to get the feeling that what I'd purchased would amount to nothing. And since I had no experience operating a donut shop, I felt lost. Nor had anyone given me any guidance; indeed, there was nothing in place to help a new franchisee—no recipes, no formulas and no operating procedures.

It was a stark contrast to the way things worked at the Dairy Queen. The most difficult part of managing that store had been to keep the equipment clean and make sure the staff were appropriately trained. Tim Hortons was also a much more labour-intensive business. Training production staff took several weeks, and being open twenty-four hours a day presented a great challenge. It was an immense amount of work, and matters were only complicated by the apparent lack of a game plan.

In those early days of the chain, customer buying patterns were very different from what they are today. Weekday sales were enough to allow us to cover all of our expenses, and customers typically came during the morning rush, often on their way to or from the nearby factories that were located a few kilometres down the road on Hamilton's waterfront. Saturday was our most popular day, as people would often come with their families and buy a dozen donuts instead of just a coffee. Sunday, with people going to church and all of the shops and workplaces closed, could often be a quiet day, but occasionally families would drop by on their way home from church.

Jim showed up not long after my call and tried to allay some of my concerns. He was a smooth talker, and those answers he did supply only addressed my questions on a superficial level. Jim always seemed to be in a rush to get somewhere else. He was certainly charming, but by this time I had serious doubts whether I could always trust what he said.

Strangely, in spite of the shoddy business practices, the store was doing okay. I wasn't unhappy with our sales, which continued to be about $1,000 per week—just as Charade had promised. I was making a reasonable living. But that figure was the only thing about Tim Hortons that I felt Charade had been honest about.

Since Jim had proven to be of little help, I decided I still needed to find a better way to make product. So I turned to our mix supplier, Jo Lowe Corporation, and asked if they had someone who might be able to give me a hand. A representative from Jo Lowe came and suggested some recipes, but they weren't successful under the conditions we faced. Through trial and error, we modified the recipes; it took

Ron Joyce

a considerable amount of time to create the appropriate mixes and product-control system. The key to making good donuts boils down to the texture of the mix. For someone who has never baked, it is quite a difficult thing to learn. You have to work by feel. Heat and humidity affect everything you do; even after you think everything is figured out, the weather could change and you are back where you started from, struggling to make a consistent product.

That was the challenge we faced with our bakers or production people, especially in the early years. How do you teach them to make a great product when a lot of it is done by feel? A good baker simply *knew* a good donut from a poor one. And good bakers were hard to come by. In the early days, once a store operator located someone who worked out, they were often poached by other stores. It got so bad that we had to institute a rule within the chain that said no one could steal someone else's baker.

Eventually, our procedures would improve, as we added illustrated manuals, training films and technical support. I will not go into the details of our production methods, but suffice it to say that our task was much more difficult because we were producing our food from scratch, and training bakers was very labour-intensive and time-consuming.

ooooo

Just as some of my fears for the shop were starting to subside, another incident cropped up that led me to question the validity of the investment. In the third week after my purchase of the store, a sheriff showed up, intent upon seizing several pieces of equipment that had not been paid for.

"There's no way you are taking my equipment," I told him forcefully. "I've paid cash for all of the items in dispute, and I can prove it."

In my opinion, it was fraud, pure and simple. Jim had given me a bill of sale or a quit claim deed to the equipment when I purchased the franchise, but Jim and Tim had not paid for it themselves and, in fact, much of the equipment they had sold to me was leased by them and they had not been making monthly payments on their contracts. This incident was the last straw. I decided it was now time to call Tim Horton and see what he knew about these issues.

I knew Tim was a hockey star, and I'd played hockey as a kid in Tatamagouche. But I'd never been to an NHL game in my life. All I knew at this point was that the Tim Horton name was on the signage and his partner appeared to be putting me on a path that could cost me my investment.

ooooo

Born in Cochrane, Ontario, in 1930, Tim played his first games in the National Hockey League during the 1949–50 season, though he didn't become a regular with the Toronto Maple Leafs for a couple of years. By the mid-1950s he had become a star defenceman, and was renowned as one of the strongest players in the league. He was equally adept at handling the puck and dishing out jarring bodychecks. Though not a tough man in the conventional sense, he was a hard-headed player and a leader in the Leafs' dressing room for almost twenty years. During his tenure in Toronto he was selected to six All-Star teams and won four Stanley Cup titles.

While he had been a great success on the ice, I would learn in time that he'd had a tougher time establishing himself away from the game of hockey. He did all kinds of things to try to supplement his hockey salary, which certainly was not very high throughout the first two decades of his career. Like many players, he would make personal appearances and sign autographs to make a little extra money. He drove a gravel truck for a while, and sold used cars. But he was always looking for a way to get ahead. I think his concern was to find something that would let him make a living when his playing days were over. In the NHL's six-team era, tales of former players who hadn't done well after their careers were finished were commonplace. And I think players like Tim were worried they would end up in the same position.

Enter Jim Charade, who convinced him to get into the restaurant business, even though Tim really didn't have any sense of how the industry worked. It was never clear to me what Tim had to do with the formation of Tim Donut Ltd., though I think he may have been involved in negotiating the lease on the Ottawa Street building.

Though he had a strong build, Tim wasn't tall; he only stood about five foot nine. This surprised me when I met him—I'd expected a more imposing figure. He also wore very thick glasses, as his eyesight was terrible. He tried wearing contacts when he played hockey, but he kept losing them when he made contact with another player. That's why he often kept his chin down towards his body—so that he wouldn't get hit in the throat if he failed to see a flying puck.

He had the brush cut that was his trademark at the time, and he wore a suit to our first meeting. His style was pretty standard for hockey players at the time—they were expected to adhere to a certain look in public. It was clear that he didn't know the business all that well and couldn't help me with any of the problems we were having. When I had operational questions, he deferred to Jim, who came to the meeting with Tim, though in hindsight, I wondered how much he knew too. Tim was enthusiastic and very trusting, and he really had a lot of faith, at least initially, in Jim. He defended Jim, but did agree that there were problems with the unpaid equipment, and promised to correct that. Tim also gave me his home phone number, and I would use it occasionally to keep him informed about the business's progress. I would also call occasionally to get tickets for Leafs games. We also agreed that we would meet on a social level, at my home on Kensington Avenue North in Hamilton.

A few weeks later, we had our first dinner with Tim and his wife, Lori. Charade and his wife, Claudette, also came to the dinner. The evening could have been tense, but instead we had fun, laughing and talking over a fine dinner and a few drinks. Tim seemed to be having a great time. (One of the unfortunate things about Tim's marriage, we would come to learn, was that Lori would often get upset with him when he appeared to be having too much fun.) Not too long after dinner finished, the Hortons decided to go home. They had arrived in Tim's Sunbeam Tiger, one of several fast sports cars Tim owned during his lifetime. This one was powered by a V-8 engine. Given that Tim had had a few drinks during the evening, Lori decided to drive home. As they drove off, it looked like Tim reached over with his foot and pushed down on the accelerator, causing the car to fishtail down the street. You could hear Lori shouting, "Tim, you're going to kill us!" Though Teri and I were not aware of it at the time, we would later learn these sorts of incidents were not uncommon with the Hortons.

Shortly after that evening, Tim made the decision that would alter his ownership role with Tim Hortons. I believe, although I wasn't privy to all of the information from the meeting, that Tim told Charade that they had to put more capital into the company to get rid of some of these outstanding problems. Jim had no further resources to invest, so he ended up losing his half of the business. Tim then transferred the shares into Lori's name, giving the Hortons full ownership in the company now called Tim Donut Ltd.*

---

* Tim Donut Ltd. would eventually have its name altered to TDL, which remains as the parent company of the Tim Hortons brand.

Since Jim was now out of the equation, some changes needed to be made to the operations. Tim had no expertise whatsoever in this area, so the burden fell squarely on my shoulders. Working with our different suppliers, we managed to put an operating plan in place.

Around that time, a second store was set to open in another renovated service station in Hamilton, at Concession and East 31st streets on top of the escarpment, south of the city's downtown core. The store's signs and the pylon with Tim's image had been installed on the building, and it had been renovated inside, but there were no equipment or furnishings of any kind. Tim and Jim's names were on the lease obligation, which meant the store had to be opened to avoid a similar fate to that of their hamburger operation, which eventually was forced into receivership.

With Charade out of the picture, Tim wanted to sell me the new store. Tim didn't have anyone else to sell to, and because the hockey season took up so much of his time, he wouldn't have had the time or the knowledge to train a new owner—especially without any operating procedures in place. At the time, I was concerned that the new store would cut into sales at the first store on Ottawa Street.

Finding the funds to buy the second store proved to be a bit of a challenge for me. I asked my mother, Grace, and her husband, Vic Annis, along with my sister, Gwen, and her husband, Gord Oliver, if they could lend me some money for a couple of years. They agreed, but to raise the rest I was forced to borrow expensive high-risk capital.

We went forward and ordered the necessary equipment and furnishings for the new store from Charlie Wood at Simpsons in Toronto. He was reluctant at first to negotiate with Tim Hortons, fearing that payment might be problematic.

"Look, I'm pretty concerned that no one at your company will be able to pay for these," Wood said, before offering a surprising twist. "But if you'll guarantee it personally, we'll release it to you." I have no idea why he made the offer, since I wasn't exactly flush with cash myself. I'd had to scramble to find the cash to acquire the store in the first place! The second store was also successful; and, far from harming the sales at the first outlet, it actually raised awareness of the Tim Hortons brand.

The biggest problem I remember having in operating the two stores was the lack of trained baking staff and of an experienced manager for the Concession Street location. This was a problem we would have to address if the company expected to sell any further franchises. With that in mind, I put together some very basic training manuals. As well, we didn't yet have any point-of-purchase materials, such as bags, boxes or uniforms, with the Tim Hortons name on them. Before I took over the first store, all of these goods had been purchased wholesale and were generic. We aimed to change that and, in the process, continue building awareness of the restaurants. The reality, of course, was that a chain with two stores didn't have much purchasing clout. While Tim received some rebates on donut mix and coffee, Tim Hortons was at the mercy of its suppliers.

The lack of organization and support became an issue that I could no longer live with. I brought it up with Tim. "I'm paying you a royalty, but I'm not getting anything for it," I told him. I suggested that perhaps it would be best if he let me buy him out and take down the Tim Hortons name.

However, Tim wasn't prepared to sell. Instead, he offered me a 10 percent stake in the business. I declined, indicating that that would not suit my needs—or his. "If I leave, you'll need someone with experience if you are going to make Tim Hortons successful," I told him.

Since we couldn't come to an agreement, I said I would move on and offered to sell him the two stores back. He refused to accept that deal, either, so my next option was to find someone else to take the stores off my hands. It did not take long to find buyers. I sold the Concession Street store to Casey and Beth Weilhower; at the same time, a friend from Tatamagouche named Ed Mattatall, with whom I'd worked at American Can, was looking to start his own business. He and his wife, Florence, purchased the Ottawa Street store.

That should have ended my association with Tim Hortons, but it didn't turn out to be that simple. By the time I had sold the second store, Tim had moved ahead with a third location, at University Avenue and Weber Street in Waterloo, Ontario, in a strip mall that also had a Dairy Queen and a variety store. The mall happened to be owned by a friend of mine, Dore Carnahan, who operated several Dairy Queens in Kitchener-Waterloo. With Tim needing to leave to join the Leafs' training camp in Peterborough in the fall of 1966, and with Charade out of the picture, there was no one in place to train, manage or operate the store. Tim contacted me and asked if I would operate it until he found somebody to buy the franchise. I reluctantly agreed, and by September, when the store opened, Tim had come to realize he had reached an impasse and couldn't continue to operate the business without help. He called me from training camp and indicated that he needed to have a partner; if I reconsidered, he said, he would sell me half the company. I drove to Peterborough and met with him. Even though I had been planning on disassociating myself from Tim Hortons, I was very excited to have the opportunity to buy into the business. Though it was still in its early stages, my feeling was that if the operation was refined and standards put in place, Tim Hortons could have a great future.

The deal was finalized just before Christmas, and I bought half the company for $12,000. Since I didn't have the money to pay Tim at the time, I agreed to take over half the debt and pay him the outstanding balance over the coming years. The arrangement saw Tim take the title of president, while I was made vice-president.

The store in Waterloo was our first grand opening. Since the first two stores had been located in Hamilton, few in Waterloo knew what a Tim Hortons was, so we aimed to generate some awareness for the new business. Tim decided to arrange for his teammates to be there, including some of the Leafs' biggest stars, like Bobby Baun, Red Kelly, Dave Keon, Frank Mahovlich and Marcel Pronovost. Despite the weather and an unpaved parking lot covered in snow, the players stayed for several hours to sign autographs. Afterwards, Tim took all the players out for dinner to thank them.

It was around this time that I recall being struck by the fact I was now a partner with one of the top hockey players in the world. Prior to meeting Tim, I had never spent much time around professional athletes, and it was hard not to be impressed. I enjoyed the camaraderie that came so easily to Tim's teammates, and I also came to have fun with the individual players. While Mahovlich was very quiet, Pronovost and Tim were both very funny, especially after they'd had a few drinks. And though we had gotten off to a rocky start, Tim and I began a strong friendship as business partners.

At the time, I didn't know the background that led to Tim's decision to make me an equal partner in the venture. When he acquired Jim Charade's part of the company in early 1965, he had given that stake to his wife, Lori. In order to make me a partner, he took Lori's portion away from her and assigned it to me. It turned out that Lori had grown quite fond of being half-owner of the business, even though she had nothing to do with it. It took Tim quite a while to convince her that it would be best to turn over her stake to me.

Finally becoming a partner in the business allowed me to begin to influence the way it was being managed. To this date, many of the ideas had been Jim's, and Tim had done little to alter them during the few months in which he operated TDL on his own. Since I had been on the front line, managing the stores, I had developed a better sense of what worked with the customers and what needed to be changed to make things more successful.

Though it caught Tim off guard, the first thing I felt we should do was drop the notion of using his hockey-player image to market the business. It struck me that the stores weren't about Tim and his position with the Toronto Maple Leafs—it was about the food we sold and whether it appealed to the customers. Regardless of whether Tim had a great year, if the donuts were not of high quality and the store wasn't clean, people wouldn't come.

"Timmy, I don't care what we call the business, but it has to have broader appeal than simply relying on hockey," I told him during one of our discussions on the business and its marketing. "If you want to call it Tim Hortons, that's fine because it's a great name, and I don't think Miles Gilbert Horton would fly. But we can't continue with the hockey image."

This ran contrary to the initial concept for the company. Jim had convinced Tim that using his image on the signs would be enough to get people through the doors and buying hamburgers in Toronto, and then donuts and coffee in Hamilton. I knew that it didn't matter whose name was on the front door if our food and coffee didn't match the customer's expectations. Besides, there were many people who didn't even know what Tim Horton looked like. In the first few years, customers would often come into the store, point at me when I was working behind the counter and say, "Look, there's Tim Horton." Needless to say, my overweight body didn't bear any resemblance to a professional athlete's physique.

It didn't take long for Tim to understand my point of view, and in the long run, I was proven correct. Today, very few people who go to the restaurants relate the Tim Hortons name to the Hall of Fame hockey player. At the same time, the company's brand recognition is the best in Canada. In fact, had we maintained the hockey image, we would have had problems with trademarks (Tim appeared on the original sign in a Maple Leafs uniform), and issues would have arisen when Tim went to play for the New York Rangers, the Pittsburgh Penguins and the Buffalo Sabres after his time in Toronto ended.

The now-famous company logo, with its two ovals, was created by a designer from Toronto, and our fourth franchise was the first to use it on its signage. At the time, I'm not sure we knew that he nailed a lasting concept; we just knew that it was better than what we had at the time. Nor did I have any idea at the time just how pervasive the Tim Hortons brand would become. There is no food-service company named after a celebrity that has reached anywhere near the prominence of the Horton brand. Several have been attempted that I recall, but they haven't succeeded because they lacked the key ingredients: operations, passion and focus. I have often reflected on the words of U.S. President Calvin Coolidge:

> *Nothing in the world can take the place of persistence.*
> *Talent will not; nothing is more common than unsuccessful men*
> *with talent.*
> *Genius will not; unrewarded genius is almost a proverb.*

Education alone will not; the world is full of educated derelicts.
Persistence and determination alone are omnipotent.

The slogan "Press on" has solved, and always will help solve, the problems facing entrepreneurship.

I also believe the quotation is an accurate reflection of why Tim Hortons would, in time, prove to be so successful.

6

REAL ESTATE AND REBATES

In the early days of Tim Donut Ltd., we worked out of Tim's home, but that proved to be a far from ideal arrangement. For one thing, we were constantly having to work around the Leafs' schedule; when Tim was on the road, things would have to be put on hold. To remedy the situation, we decided to rent a small office in Oakville, Ontario, which was roughly halfway between our two homes. Tim Horton was not only one of the finest hockey players in the world, he was an honest business partner. And, perhaps because of all the problems he'd had with Jim and other associates, he demanded a level of trust from our arrangement. This was reflected in the way we furnished the office: Tim insisted that our desks face one another, so that we would always be able to look each other in the eye while speaking.

Like me, Tim was better equipped when it came to street smarts and common sense than education. He'd grown up playing hockey and, aside from his forays into various side businesses, had been focused on sports for his entire adult life. Given the demands that that life placed upon him, aside from real-estate acquisitions or leases, he didn't have the business skills or the time our developing young chain required.

Following the opening of our third store (we ended up selling the franchise to Pat McGrinder, a police officer I knew from Hamilton, and his wife, also named Pat), we planned to slow down and assess the business and its fundamentals. We didn't open another store that year. By this time, I had come to several conclusions about Tim Donut Ltd. I became convinced that the business's success depended on the freshness of the product. And my standards were especially strict: I didn't want production to start until 3 a.m. (continuing until 11:30 a.m.), though some might have preferred to make the donuts earlier and let them sit on shelves longer. Freshness was my mantra, but it was difficult to find employees willing to start work in the wee hours. I had gotten the baking down to a science and could make dozens of donuts by myself, but that resulted in another complication. Lacking my experience, trainees had to start earlier to make the same amount of product. Besides which, it was hot, difficult work that few were willing to undertake.

As mentioned, despite our limited budget and buying power, I determined early on to use our boxes and cups to start marketing the Tim Hortons brand. We made the best of what we could afford, and as we grew, we found new ways to make those cups even more of a marketing tool: by the 1970s, we were using cups with seasonal logos, like Christmas cups, throughout the chain. In many ways this was the precursor to the "Roll Up the Rim" campaign that would be launched nearly twenty years later. Even the signs near the street were a big factor—they drew people in and encouraged impulse purchasing.

We also created a consistent image for all of our stores. We decorated them in warm colours like maroon and gold—we learned early on that "cold" colours, like the Leafs' blue and white, wouldn't work for us. Countertops were gold, while stools were red. Continuing with this theme, we also chose low-power lighting rather than cold, bright fluorescents. There was no model for us to work from, but Tim was very keen on the design element of the stores. He personally picked out the "blue steel" brick that we used for many of the stores; he had used the same brick for his home in the Toronto suburb of Willowdale that he had built himself.

While business issues dominated my thinking throughout most of 1966, I also came to realize that I needed a steady source of income, especially since I no longer owned the first two Tim Hortons stores. With my committed focus to the company, I had become less dedicated to the Dairy Queen, so I decided to sell it. By this time, I was commuting daily into Hamilton and Waterloo from Stoney Creek, where Teri and I lived. Only at this point did we consider opening a fourth store. Since there was no way Tim Donut could afford to pay me a salary given the meagre royalties the three stores were paying, we determined it would be best if I managed the fourth store in order to secure an income.

Once we decided to go forward with a fourth store, a location had to be found. I visited a site on King Street West in Hamilton, and it was clear to me that it would be ideal for our new store. However, there was a catch: I couldn't get the owner of the land, a man named Sy Freedman, to agree to build the restaurant and lease it back to us. Freedman was, however, amenable to leasing the land to us at a rate of $100 a month, increasing by $25 per month each year. While that didn't immediately look like such a great suggestion, Freedman told me that at the end of five years, all the rent increases would go against purchasing the land, which was valued at $25,000, outright. It turns out that Freedman had been one of the partners in the produce business that I'd driven a truck for when I was a police officer. He liked my work ethic, and it inspired him to offer us this special deal. We hadn't planned on this, our first foray into real estate, but in the years to come it would be central to Tim Hortons' success. The arrangement wasn't without its hiccups: it turns out that some local residents caught wind of the deal and objected, as they had been using the land for local beautification efforts. But Sy had some pull locally and was able to obtain a building permit.

After the 1966–67 hockey season, Tim decided he was going to hold out for a better contract rather than report to training camp in Peterborough as he typically did each September. As he often did during the last years of his career, he threatened retirement, and would claim that his work at Tim Hortons was demanding most of his time. Hockey was secondary to the donut business, he'd tell Maple Leafs management, though I knew that was not actually the case.

In the meantime, Tim determined that he would build the new store on King Street himself. He always enjoyed construction work, and he was insistent that he should act as the project's general contractor. One rainy day, he was wearing rubber boots and dressed for the task at hand. While he prepared to pour the footings, a group of school-age children and their teacher walked past the construction site on their way to the library.

One of the kids recognized Tim.

"Teacher," the student said, pointing at Tim, "there's Tim Horton."

"Yes, I know," she said. "And if you don't go to school, you'll end up digging ditches just like him."

Tim continued to hold out, even after the construction of the building was well under way. The media began to ask why Tim, who at this time was a Second Team All-Star as well as a member of a Stanley Cup–winning team, wasn't coming back to play hockey. The answer was always the same: "I have a donut business to run."

Eventually, Stafford Smythe, part of the Leafs' ownership group, wrote Tim a nasty letter telling him it was unprincipled to ignore his contract. Soon after he received the letter, Tim came into one of the stores while I was baking in the kitchen. It was near the end of a run of donuts and there was a lot of scrap product around to be thrown out. Tim took some of the scraps, put them in a Tim Hortons box and gift-wrapped it. He addressed it to Punch Imlach, who was coaching the Leafs at training camp in Peterborough at the time, with a note: "Punch: With donuts like these, who needs hockey?"

But as he always did, Tim went back to hockey, this time doubling the amount of his previous contract to $42,500 per year. But the Leafs were not the same after their Stanley Cup win in 1967, and Tim, who was making a lot of money for an aging star, became expendable. By the spring of 1970 he would be headed to New York to play for the Rangers.

Despite continuing to play hockey, in the off-seasons he still helped with the construction of new restaurants. When we prepared to open our seventh store in Stoney Creek, just outside of Hamilton, Tim was in charge of making sure the store was furnished appropriately. While we had developed a fairly standard layout for our stores, in Stoney Creek the usual plan would have left the restaurant facing a building. So, we decided to flip the plans so it would face a park. I made a point of reminding Tim about this decision, since he usually purchased the fixtures for the store, and much of it would have to be altered to accommodate the new setup.

We were under a tight schedule and we needed to watch our cash. The day the equipment arrived, it was clear that Tim had never told anyone about the change of plans. The two franchise owners, Ed Mattatall and Casey Wellhower, were preparing to open the store on a very tight budget, and the situation was a disaster. I called Tim and was pretty angry about the miscommunication.

"I told you to ensure our fixture people flipped the plans," I said over the phone, before going into some detail about how upset I was. Tim paused for a moment before answering.

Then he said, "I'll tell you what I'll do, Ron. I'll drive down to the Skyway Bridge and jump off, or I can order new equipment. What do you think I should do?"

It was just an example of how he could bring perspective to any crisis. In that respect, he was a great counterpoint to me, as I often took everything too seriously. Of course, the situation didn't do much for our credibility with the franchise owners.

∞∞∞

A shortage of capital would be a huge obstacle for the company, one that wouldn't be alleviated in the slightest until 1975. One of the ways we tried to deal with this was by striking deals with our suppliers. For instance, whenever we opened a new store, we needed to purchase equipment. I knew only too well that we needed to avoid a repeat of the sheriff's visit to the first store, but we still weren't able to buy the equipment outright. Fortunately for us, our suppliers were anxious to have us buy more products from them, and in exchange, they would lend us the money to acquire the needed equipment. Though it sounds unusual, it is a time-honoured practice that was even used during the recent boom in the technology and telecommunications markets. The arrangement allowed us to sell the equipment to the new store owner as part of the franchise agreement. Typically, however, we didn't immediately pay the money back to the suppliers; instead, we used it to help further our expansion. It worked well for many years of the company, until one of our suppliers brought in new management who felt the practice was too speculative. They were probably right—if Tim Hortons had failed, it would have cost them a great deal of money.

The future of the business depended on our ability to grow the franchise system. But that meant raising more money, and traditional lenders—banks and credit unions—refused us, claiming the venture was unproven. That forced us to borrow from some very expensive sources. Some of these creditors often charged 20 percent interest on the money they offered us; other loans came with front-end commissions attached. In other words, if we borrowed $20,000 to launch a new store, we would only actually receive $17,000, since there was a $3,000 "fee" charged back on the loan. Unfortunately, you still owed the lender the entire principal of $20,000. As our debts mounted, it was all we could do to keep our heads above water. It still amazes me, but we never defaulted on any of our loans during that time of growth.

Tim once approached Harold Ballard, then one of the owners of the Leafs, and asked if he could borrow $20,000. Ballard trusted Tim, but wouldn't lend him the money. Instead, he told Tim to see his banker and borrow the money and Ballard would co-sign the loan. We had to be creative, and some of the arrangements we made were far from ideal for a growing business, but this was how we were able to continue buying land and building stores in the first few years.

By the fifth store opening in December 1967—in a great location on Plains Road in Burlington, operated by Eldon and Doreen Fawcett—we knew the chain was starting to gather momentum and customers were beginning to relate to the brand. The scene at the opening was akin to the scenes of pandemonium that were witnessed in 2001 at the openings of Krispy Kreme stores in Canada. Our grand opening was held on a rainy, muddy day, but that didn't deter the customers, who packed the store. Once again, Tim had recruited his teammates to help kick things off. Though the interest in Tim Hortons was growing, adding the Leaf players to the mix, many of whom were the biggest stars in the game at the time, meant the store was packed with customers. I recall walking around the muddy, unpaved parking lot giving away trays of hot donuts to the throng of people waiting to get autographs. One kid was so excited to see Frank Mahovlich that he grabbed Frank's coat and tried to climb up his back—wearing his muddy shoes; Frank was stunned and uncertain what to do. The store is still at the same location today, and for a long time after it opened it was the most successful restaurant in the area, thriving even as several well-known American chains opened and closed very quickly.

Store number 6 was at Upper James Street and Mohawk Road in Hamilton, and this was our most expensive location to date. We paid $50,000 for the land, and we had to do a lot of work on the site before we could build the store. I had to convince Tim it would be our best location. This store was sold to Al and Pat Murray, whom I'd worked with at Firestone years before—Al was also from Tatamagouche. We had a grand opening on a hot, humid day in August. We'd promoted it well, considering our limited budget, and there were many NHL players on hand.

That day turned out to be a financial disaster for us. We had made a lot of product ahead of time to keep up with the expected demand, and instead we were hosts to a very empty parking lot. My credibility with Tim, Al and Pat took a big hit. But we learned a lesson from this experience, about how weather affected business. This store would become our highest-volume location for many years to come, and Al and Pat went on to own multiple stores and prospered financially, thanks to a huge commitment of time and effort.

Store number 8 in Brantford was another land purchase, and we sold this store to Don and Donna Pritlove. This store, although small, broke new records upon opening and is still doing very well almost forty years later. Store number 9 in Cambridge was another land purchase and build. This store was purchased by George and Dorothy McGlinchey, from St. Stephen, New Brunswick; I'd met George while we were moonlighting from our jobs on the police department and at Stelco. He and I drove produce trucks for Netkin's and were paid a dollar an hour. The store was very successful for them, and they also became multiple-store owners.

As you can see, except for Casey and Beth, all of these early stores were sold to friends and acquaintances of mine. One thing we all had in common was the desire for a better life, and we were not afraid to work hard or put in long hours to obtain it. Most of the people from the first ten stores are still involved in the business today.

This growth put a certain amount of pressure on our small but functional head office on North Service Road in Oakville. After a couple of years, Tim came into the office and announced he'd bought us a new building. It was an old Salvation Army church at 135 Trafalgar Road in Oakville that had been abandoned. There was a Victorian house next door, which was over 100 years old, that came as part of the deal. We bulldozed the church, and used the house as our office. We moved to the office in 1970 and opened store number 17, a small store which served as the first training centre. It was too small to allow us to actually do a lot of training, but it did allow us to show prospective owners just how the stores operated. The house worked well as our office, but we were only there for a couple of years before we moved to Sinclair Road, where the current office and warehouse stand.

Despite the success of restaurants like the one on Plains Road, definite problems were showing up in the way Jim Charade had set up the franchise system for Tim Hortons. It didn't take long to realize we couldn't afford to add stores and pay interest rates of 20 percent if we were only making 3 percent of gross sales—which was only slightly better than the 2 percent Jim and Tim had started out collecting—and a small percentage to cover advertising costs. By this time the stores were often grossing $2,500 per week in revenue, or about $130,000 in annual sales, but the royalty they paid didn't cover the capital costs. I had been told by others in the restaurant industry that for a franchise operation to really succeed, a royalty rate of 10 percent was necessary. Clearly, we were falling way short.

There were four ways to generate cash flow in the franchise business: the initial sale price of the franchise; the royalties collected from ongoing franchises; negotiating volume discounts with suppliers; and, of course, rental income.

Of these, I saw real estate as the most attractive option. The germ of this idea had been planted when we made the land deal with Sy Freedman for the King Street store in Hamilton. It occurred to me that if Tim Donut Ltd. acquired the land and built the store, we could lease the building to the franchisee. Under the new system I set up, a franchisee who operated a store on land we owned would pay us a flat rent, or a percentage of gross sales, whichever was greater. We started off at 7 percent of gross sales, but as we expanded and entered into larger and more expensive real-estate transactions, the rate gradually increased to 10 percent.

In the first few years of Tim Hortons, there were numerous critics who said the real-estate strategy would fail and said I was crazy to pursue it. And Tim was among them. He felt it was too risky and would prove the company's undoing, especially since we were cannibalizing Tim Hortons' cash flow to continue acquiring properties. Had the chain added enough operations that didn't meet expectations, the company could have become overextended and the strategy might have proven disastrous. Instead, over the years it turned out to be one of the company's greatest sources of revenue. Many of our competitors, especially Canadian franchise operations, did not invest in real estate in the same way, and they still struggle with cash flow because of it.

Our financial issues delayed our entry into the Toronto market. Though it only made sense that the company would eventually try to tackle Canada's largest market after our success in southern Ontario, we were reluctant to try it. Five years and twenty stores after we opened the first store on Ottawa Street, you still couldn't find a Tim Hortons in Metropolitan Toronto. Maybe it was a holdover from his terrible experience with the hamburger restaurants, but Tim never seemed keen on pushing into the city that had made him famous. To some observers, it might have seemed natural for a Leafs star to do business in Toronto. Using Jim Charade's logic and Tim's name, moving into the market might have seemed like a natural fit, but there were also a number of obvious drawbacks. First of all, Toronto was, even then, an expensive city, and although Tim Hortons was growing, we were still far from flush. Secondly, the market was getting crowded, with Mister Donut and Country Style already competing for the coffee-and-donut dollar.

In 1969 I was approached by a man who wanted to partner with us. His company had already opened several stores that sold hamburgers and donuts under the name Friar Tuck's. Though I rebuffed his initial offers, he still wanted to meet Tim and me at his Toronto office.

"You can own 100 percent of a small operation, or you can be partners in a much bigger one," he urged during a phone conversation. Following his call, we decided to see what he might be able to bring to the table.

The meeting was an unusual one. After arriving at the fellow's office in Toronto, we were ushered into a boardroom that contained a table and six or seven telephones. As soon as the prospective partner began speaking to us, a phone would ring and he'd pick it up, listen for a minute and bark, "Sell." Another phone would ring, and he'd go through the same process, this time shouting "Buy" before hanging up. It was really odd, but I'm sure it was supposed to impress the hockey player and ex-cop he was meeting with. I remember Tim and I were suspicious that it was in fact his secretary making all the calls to the room.

"There's no way we are doing business with this person," Tim told me as soon as we left the meeting. Neither his partnership with Tim Donut Ltd. nor his business model actually came to fruition. He would end up charged with fraud and his restaurants were closed. Soon afterwards, the landlord who controlled two of the properties contacted us and asked whether we might be interested in taking over the locations.

"Ron, let's stay out of Toronto," Tim told me when we discussed the matter. "It is just too tough a market." Despite Tim's hesitation, we went ahead and acquired two stores in Toronto.

Given our success to that point with stores in Hamilton, Kitchener-Waterloo, Welland, Brantford and Cambridge, etc., I suppose I was beginning to feel as if bullets would bounce off my chest and that anything we touched would turn to gold. That wasn't the case with the two Toronto stores. Even with the Tim Hortons brand attached to them, we had a hard time convincing customers to forget the earlier problems Tim's stores had faced. The stores lost money, and we had to forgive royalties and switch franchise owners just to try to keep them afloat. Eventually the restaurant at Lawrence and Brimley in Scarborough succumbed to poor sales, and for the first time in the chain's history we had to close a store. However, the second, on The Queensway in Etobicoke, was successful and remains open to this day. If Tim was annoyed about the fact that I went ahead with the Toronto stores despite his misgivings, I never heard about it. He rarely voiced any unhappiness about the way I ran the operation, though he would occasionally become annoyed that, in the interests of expanding the chain, I continued to spend more money than we were taking in.

ooooo

The failure in Toronto taught us an important lesson. We focused our efforts on the smaller cities where we had already experienced success. In retrospect, and though it wasn't planned this way at the time, it was a smart business move for us to operate in these smaller communities. Though they lacked Toronto's massive population base, we could tap into them without a massive advertising push, which was something we couldn't have afforded at the time anyway. Secondly, we benefited from being a big name in a smaller market; a new franchise might have become lost in a larger city like Toronto or Montreal.

We also felt we understood what the small towns wanted from Tim Hortons. As a result, most of our competitors, who were vying for spots in the largest cities, essentially conceded markets like Kingston, Brantford, Stoney Creek, Cornwall, Belleville, Brockville and Sudbury to us, which gave us a great foothold from which to expand. Other operators in the food-service industry thought this sort of strategy was destined to fail, but we proved them wrong.

I also believe we benefited when we finally made another move into Toronto. In Canada, people often grow up in smaller towns and cities and then move to the larger centres to find employment. These people grew up with our coffee and donuts, and when they moved to places like Toronto, they were looking for the familiar, which was what we offered. In many ways I think that for many Canadians in the 1980s and '90s, Tim Hortons was like a touch of home.

This concept also yielded strange results every so often. On one occasion in the mid-1970s, I received a phone call late at night.

"Is this Ron Joyce, the owner of Tim Hortons?" a man's voice asked. I told him it was. I didn't wonder about how he obtained my number until after the call was through.

"Well, Mr. Joyce, I live in Calgary and I have a problem. I used to live in Hamilton and have moved out west recently."

I wasn't sure where he was going with this confession, but I was intrigued enough not to hang up the phone.

"Well, you've got me hooked on Tim Hortons coffee and now I'm in Calgary and I can't find any of your stores here. I'm wondering what you are going to do about it."

I told him I'd see what I could do, and thanked him politely for the call. It would be another few years before we expanded into Calgary (the first store in Alberta, located in Red Deer, opened in 1979, while store number 124 opened in Calgary a year later), but the call demonstrated the appeal Tim Hortons was beginning to have for customers not just in Ontario, but across Canada. By the time Tim Hortons had been in business for fifteen years, generations of people in Ontario had come to make us a part of their everyday lives. Incidentally, the caller's mention of being "hooked" on our coffee raises another topic: for many years, there have been rumours and urban legends that claim we add something to our coffee—whether it's nicotine, mono-sodium glutamate or a higher-than-normal amount of caffeine—to render it addictive. That simply isn't the case. In 2004, the CBC program *Disclosure* actually sent samples of coffee to a lab. Not only was the lab unable to detect any unusual substances, but it found that TH coffee has less caffeine than many of its competitors' products.

∞∞∞

As mentioned earlier, the other way we made money in the early years of the company was through volume discounts, also know as the rebate system. Though it was a common practice in the industry, I always felt uncomfortable with it. In a nutshell, the parent company would nego-tiate with a supplier, getting a substantial volume discount in exchange for a promise to buy the supplier's product exclusively. The franchisees were then charged as if the volume discount had not been negotiated. The franchisor would pocket the difference—in other words, the parent company would not pass the savings on to the franchise owner. It was an important source of income for Tim Donut, given the low royalty rates we were charging at the time.

However, the issue became quite contentious as the 1960s drew to a close. In Canada, the first important battle between a chain and its franchisees began in 1971, in the famous Jirna Ltd. case against Mister Donut. The suit raised the question of who should receive the benefits of rebates from suppliers. Jirna was the operator of Mister Donut franchises in Toronto, and it felt it should be entitled to the commissions and rebates Mister Donut was extracting from its suppliers. Jirna's lawyers argued that the rebate system wasn't fair, even though it was set out in their franchise agreement.

We became even more concerned when Jirna won its case; the

judgment concluded that the franchisee was entitled to thousands of dollars in damages for misrepresentations made by Mister Donut. The case was appealed, and the decision was overturned in 1975, but when the original judgment was handed down we had no way of knowing which way things would turn. By 1971, we had twenty-five stores operating throughout Ontario, from Cambridge in the west to Cornwall in the east, and plans were in the works for stores to open as far north as North Bay. I felt there could be trouble ahead for Tim Hortons if we continued to use the rebate system.

My concerns led me to approach the owners of our twenty-five stores about ending the practice at Tim Hortons. "Look," I told them, "we'll get out of the rebate system, but in exchange, we'll look to raise the overall royalty to 6 percent from 3 percent." I fully expected they'd take the deal, especially when I explained to them how they would benefit. "In exchange, we'll negotiate the best price with suppliers and pass the cost savings onto you."

But I couldn't convince them that the proposal was in their best interest. They wouldn't budge from the deals they had initially signed. Instead, they formed an owners' association and started talking to lawyers. Tim was not happy about my meetings with the franchise owners, and felt I had exposed our inner workings. On the other hand, I was concerned that we could actually lose the company. It looked like the Jirna case all over again. Since we were reinvesting all of our cash flow into expansion, losing a lawsuit would probably be the end of the company as we knew it. And the notion that the owners, who were largely friends that I had helped get into the business, would take legal action against us was really distressing to me personally.

I knew that some of the owners who started the association were not honouring their franchise agreements to the letter. In fact, a number of them were operating stores that did not meet the standards for freshness and cleanliness called for in their contracts. "Okay, gentlemen, you've got an association," I told them in one of our meetings, "but you'd better be prepared. Because I'm going to enforce every part of our franchise agreements." Despite the tough talk, I knew the threat of pulling their franchises would not keep them from going forward with legal action in the long run.

"Tim, we've got to see if we can restructure the company and get out of the rebate business altogether," I told him emphatically. But the idea of dumping the rebate system would come with harsh financial repercussions. We simply couldn't afford to continue operating at a 3 percent royalty, which would not allow the system to be readily expanded. That led me to consider our options, and eventually I determined that we should cut out the middleman and start our own distribution centre. This would not only free us from the rebate system, but open up a new stream of cash flow.

I wanted to introduce a one-stop shop and cut out the middlemen who delivered our product from the supplier to the stores. I had set my sights on creating a central distribution operation for Tim Hortons that would supply all of the stores in the chain. If we delivered our own product to the stores, we would be entitled to a reasonable mark-up on the supplies without fearing that the franchise owners would launch court challenges as they had against Mister Donut. There was also the potential for the distribution centre's profits to outpace what we had made by using volume pricing. Of course, our risk was also higher, because we would have to invest in the equipment and buildings needed to collect and distribute the supplies.

Tim didn't agree with me at first. I think he had a tough time seeing the big picture for the business in the way I perceived it. But our partnership arrangement meant I had to have Tim's approval before going forward. Partly to convince Tim of the validity of the idea, I proposed that we would label everything with the Tim Hortons brand. That meant all of the product we would ship, right down to the trucks that would move the supplies, would have the Tim Hortons logo on it.

I finally managed to convince Tim of the strength of the concept in 1970 when he was living in New York and playing for the Rangers. We bought land at 874 Sinclair Road in Oakville, which became the new home of our head office as well as the site of our first distribution centre. To raise the capital for this endeavor, we decided to ask two friends, Layton Coulter and Ken Gariepy, if they wished to be part of the investment opportunity, specifically the land acquisition (4.5 acres) and new warehouse and offices. They agreed to become equal partners with Tim and me, with the expectation we would develop the property further and lease to other tenants. In retrospect, the second part never happened as the property was rapidly developed into the new distribution centre, and the newest training centre quickly expanded. The site is still the head office for the company today. The warehouse and offices were expanded several times over the years, and today the entire building has been transformed into the chain's head office. We eventually purchased a large parcel of land across the road, where the new warehouse and training facility are located.

The move to become our own distributor also turned us into a trucking company. TDL was a pioneer in this respect in the Canadian food-service industry. On the plus side, this meant that we could paint our rolling stock with the Tim Hortons logo and pictures of our food offerings. In a sense, they became moving billboards for the company. The first truck we purchased was a GMC straight rig with an automatic transmission. It was a mechanical disaster. It was continually breaking down at the worst possible times; needless to say, we were not pleased at the thought of a disabled truck proudly displaying our logos and colours for all to see. One Friday afternoon, the truck had one of its breakdowns on Toronto's Gardiner Expressway, blocking traffic. We received a letter from an entrepreneurial leasing company the next week. He wrote, "What's a four letter word ending in 'k' that sounds like truck?" He proceeded to say that they had seen our vehicle broken down on the Gardiner and would like to know if we were interested in leasing some of their equipment. We didn't take them up on their offer!

The distribution model turned out to be a massive success and would expand as Tim Hortons moved to other provinces. The Oakville warehouse continued to grow with the chain and in the early 1990s there were enough stores in Ontario to warrant a second facility to serve the eastern part of the province as well as Quebec. In 1979, we opened a second warehouse in Moncton, New Brunswick, to service the Atlantic provinces, and eight years later we opened facilities in Calgary and in Langley, British Columbia, to look after the western provinces. When I reflect upon the success of Tim Hortons, I think the distribution centres are an integral part of what we're all about. They represent one of the company's many successful milestones and are still one of the central revenue streams for the chain today.

7

THE LAST DAYS OF THE PARTNERSHIP

By late 1973 TDL had come to a crossroads. Tim and I were split on how the chain should go forward, and both of us had very different ideas about which regions of Canada to start developing next.

Perhaps the fact that I grew up in Nova Scotia made expansion into Atlantic Canada seem like the obvious choice. Though the region was separated from Ontario by the large province of Quebec, it seemed feasible to build stores in New Brunswick and Nova Scotia without too much difficulty.

Tim wasn't as bullish about that notion, preferring to make a stab at British Columbia. His thinking was clear: Vancouver was a wealthier part of Canada and people would have more disposable income.

In the end, we decided to proceed in both directions. Land in the Vancouver area was very expensive, so we settled on a piece of property in suburban Richmond for our first store in the province. In contrast, real estate was much more affordable in the Maritimes. We settled on

Moncton, New Brunswick, as our first location, as the city is considered by many to be the hub of Atlantic Canada. A lot was purchased on Mountain Road for $35,000 in January 1974. When our bid was accepted, it was a big thrill for me; I was convinced that we were headed in a very successful direction. I was so pleased that I called Tim that night—he was in Buffalo, at the Hilton—to deliver the news. I'm not sure Tim ever understood why this store was so important to us. Three days later, we acquired our first location in Nova Scotia, on Wyse Road in Dartmouth.

The Moncton franchise was sold to Gary O'Neill, an acquaintance from Hamilton who came from our hometown of Tatamagouche, and his wife, Mary. Like me, Gary's father, Carl, had moved to Ontario to look for employment, and in the early 1970s Gary approached us and said he was interested in operating a franchise. But it wasn't clear where he would come up with the needed capital. He continued to persist about being allowed to acquire a franchise, but the answer was always the same: "Gary, you just don't have the money to do this. We're purchasing the land and putting up the building, so we need someone who can pay cash for the franchise." But he was insistent, eventually selling his home so that he could come up with the down payment needed to acquire the location. Though I wasn't sure he could afford it, I liked Gary. He was my sort of guy—hard-working and willing to take big risks to chase his dream. Though we knew his finances would be tight, we agreed to let him open the store, which was number 43 in the system.

Though I had been so supportive of the notion of opening on Canada's east coast, I knew there was a risk that the Tim Hortons phenomenon would not translate outside of Ontario. Donuts were common in Atlantic Canada, but they paled in comparison to the selection and quality of what we offered. Still, people constantly told me we would have to alter our products in order to make a dent in the market. They wanted us to offer the same kinds of donuts and coffee that were typically offered in eastern Canada, but I balked. We would either succeed or fail with the same format we had developed in Ontario. The distance between the Moncton store and our operations in Ontario was also an issue.

My faith was rewarded when the store finally opened and there were huge lineups of people looking to try our food and coffee. The store would go on to achieve the highest volume in the chain, and Moncton would become a hub for our operations in eastern Canada. Store number 44 was opened two weeks later, and was owned by my brother Bill. It became the store with the second-highest volume, next to Gary's operation. Bill was a Runyonesque character who loved to gamble and live life to its fullest. He was fascinated by boxing and, later in his life, would travel to Las Vegas for fights. He had followed me to Ontario when he was seventeen, after a falling-out with our stepfather. He bounced around for a while before moving to Oshawa and getting married. For much of the time he was in Oshawa, he operated as a professional gambler and ran underground gaming establishments. I went to a couple of his games in those years, but I'd get cleaned out in no time; I was no match for the characters who came to Bill's games. Eventually, his tendencies caught up with him and he lost his nest egg. That forced him to consider his options, and he turned to me in the hope of entering the donut business. I had no problem helping him start with Tim Hortons, but I told him he had to put the gambling behind him.

After he went through the training, Bill took over a store in St. Catharines for us. In 1974, he heard we were planning the store in

Dartmouth, and asked if he could operate it. The only problem was that he didn't have the capital to purchase the franchise. We manoeuvred around that issue by letting him come on board through what was referred to as an "80/20" deal: he operated the store, while TDL took 20 percent of the sales. The deal worked for a few years, and then he purchased the store outright.

Of course, he never truly gave up gambling and, as I always figured he would, he returned to it later in life. But he was a hustler and an entrepreneur. In Halifax, he developed a business selling donuts and coffee directly to the navy ships. Of course, he didn't report any of these sales to me or to TDL. I knew it was going on, but the company looked the other way. After all, we were still making money shipping all the ingredients and packaging that was used in the production and he wasn't the only one not reporting all the sales to avoid paying royalties and other charges. Bill did well enough to end up with four stores. He died in 1997, after struggling for years with his health. By that time, he had sold his stores back to the chain.

While the stores in Dartmouth and Moncton prospered, our concept for western Canada was less successful. It would take four years before we opened for business in British Columbia.

We also made a mistake in bypassing the Quebec market. Henry Svazas, our vice-president in charge of real-estate development for the company at the time, didn't think we would be successful there, given the additional costs associated with translating everything into French. I didn't agree; I felt the concept would work in Quebec and would prove to be a strategic extension of our stores in eastern Ontario. In retrospect, I wasn't firm enough about my interest in pursuing the idea.

ooooo

While the chain was undergoing a risky expansion, Tim's life was also changing. He was in Buffalo, playing for Punch Imlach after being traded from the Pittsburgh Penguins.

Two years earlier, when Tim had signed with Pittsburgh, he suggested that, since we were equal partners, we should share his salary. I'm not sure why he came to this decision, but it is my feeling that he was interested in continuing in hockey in some capacity after he retired as a player and was aware that he would not be able to dedicate himself full time to TDL. Some have questioned whether I pressured him into giving up his salary as part of the deal, since his deals after leaving the Leafs were quite substantial, including a $150,000 one-year contract with Buffalo for the 1973–74 season. But that simply wasn't the case. His rationale was that in taking the same salary in the company, he felt it would be fair to include, and share, his hockey salary. At the time, each of us was drawing an annual salary of $35,000 from Tim Hortons, plus a car. The portion of his salary that would typically have been paid in tax was then lent to TDL as a loan to finance the expansion of the company. TDL would then repay this money at a later date.

As time passed, Tim became far less involved in the day-to-day operations of TDL. Looking back on those days, I came to appreciate that Tim also wanted some downtime. Ever since he was a kid, he'd worked, whether it was at hockey or holding an additional job in the off-season. He had married Lori when he was young and started a family, so he'd always supplemented his hockey income with off-season work. At the end of his career, hockey had become a job, and the salary he made from it, coupled with the fact the company was doing well, gave him a degree of freedom. He was quite happy with the team we had put together and didn't feel the need to be involved in every facet of the operation.

That didn't mean he didn't occasionally try to learn some aspects of the business. In the summer of 1971, he decided that when Lori and his four daughters went up to a rental cottage in Port Carling, he would learn to make donuts.

"Ron, I want you to teach me how to bake," he explained.

"Okay," I said. "I can do this, but we'll need two weeks and I'll put you through the entire process, just like a store owner. It'll be one-on-one training."

He agreed. The first night he came in turned out to be a bit of a disaster. The space where the baking was done was quite small and restrictive. And the donuts were fried in vegetable oil that was heated to 360 degrees Fahrenheit. In order to prepare the donuts properly, you placed them on wire screens and dunked them in the oil to fry for about two minutes. Then you took metal lifters and used them to pick up the screens and lift the donuts out of the fryer. It was difficult, but most people would quickly get the hang of it.

During training, I expected the baker to make 100 pounds of yeast-based donuts, and then the white and chocolate cake donuts, as well as the French crullers. The idea was to be able to do this within eight hours. The goal would be 200 dozen, at the very least. That was the standard we tried to create with the owners and bakers. It was enough to get through the rush. But in order to do it, you needed a very disciplined schedule. Keeping up with the yeast as it would rise was the challenge, and you needed to manage your time in order to pull it off. A good baker could proof, cut dough and fry donuts at the same time. Given the demands, the kitchens in our restaurants were usually quite small, so the baker did not need to move very far. They were designed to be cost-effective and very efficient. But that also meant the kitchens were very hot.

With all of this in mind, it isn't surprising that Tim had difficulty with baking right from the start. Once he picked up the screen with the wooden blocks, it started sliding towards him. In order to stop it from falling, he used his biceps to stop the screen. The problem was that the screen was still very hot from being in the oil and he burned himself badly. By the end of the night, his upper arms were covered in small burns. Burning yourself while baking is a bit of a rite of passage; I'd burned myself so many times working at the first store that I didn't even notice it after a few weeks.

On the second night, Tim showed up and we went to work. At about 3 a.m., Tim's former teammate Dave Keon and another player showed up. Tim had told Dave that he was making donuts, and Keon had come in to witness this. They laughed as soon as they saw Tim and gave him a hard time about wearing the white baker's outfit. On the third night, Tim never showed up. That was the end of his training. The problem was that I'd given the baker two weeks off, so now I had to run the place on my own. That was the extent of Tim's training in the business; occasionally he would get behind the counter to serve coffee, but that was only for photo opportunities.

In contrast, I continued to work occasionally in the restaurants for years after I became partners with Tim. In the 1960s, I would regularly work Sunday nights at the store I ran, because business was slow and it allowed me to do the books. If a customer came in, I'd serve them, but after midnight few customers stopped in.

Still, Tim remained interested in the real-estate component of the company. When we would find a location that might work for a new restaurant, Tim was brought in to consider the numbers. Every offer we made to purchase or lease property was conditional on the approval of the other partner.

As he withdrew from the business, Tim's personality mellowed, though I was never certain why. Tim had always liked to party. He wasn't an alcoholic, by any stretch of the imagination, but his drinking was probably a contributing factor to the problems he faced in his marriage. I never spoke with him about it, but there were rumours that, in the summer of 1972, he'd had a heated disagreement with Lori at the cottage that led to the police being called. Whatever the truth may be, it soon became apparent that he was a changed man. He seemed quieter, even withdrawn, after that summer. Despite the change in his personality, the relationship with Lori, which had been rocky as long as I'd known them, remained largely unaltered and dysfunctional.

ooooo

By the summer of 1973, there was some discussion of Tim finally giving up hockey and joining me in the business full time. It was clear that Tim wasn't as interested in playing hockey as he had been when he was younger and, at age forty-three, he was slowing down. His end-to-end rushes, which he was famous for early in his career, were largely a thing of the past. He hung around the blue line a lot more, simply because it meant he wouldn't get beaten heading back into his team's end. He was still very strong—with huge legs—and that made it difficult for the other team's forwards to get by him. Despite the fact he was well past his prime, Punch Imlach felt he was a great mentor in the dressing room for the Sabres. Punch had a lot of young players on his team in 1973–74, so even though Tim had planned to retire, Punch managed to talk him into coming back to act as a steadying force for the Sabres.

Though we often spoke of him putting the game behind him, I'm not sure he was ever committed to the idea. More than anything else, he enjoyed the camaraderie of his teammates. At the same time, being on the road kept him away from the uneasiness of having to deal with Lori on a daily basis. Their marriage had gone beyond being difficult, and Lori would occasionally even go as far as to write management to complain about their treatment of Tim. To many, it appeared that Tim could have been much further ahead if Lori had stayed uninvolved in his hockey career. In order to deal with Tim, you got Lori, too—it was a package deal. Many people wouldn't deal with Tim because of that fact.

A player's wife can be an asset or a liability. Lori was the latter, and you never knew when she'd explode. She was an attention seeker and simply loved to be at the centre of every conversation and social outing. But Tim was the star and he was the person that most of the people wanted to be with, which often led to awkward situations. Lori would dominate a conversation while Tim sat there quietly.

She was also occasionally in hospital, though Tim would never tell me what she was being treated for. It later became clear that Lori had a problem with amphetamines and other medications, though I did not know this at the time. Occasionally she'd come to social events and she'd barely be able to walk. I knew something was up, but I was never certain exactly what the problem was. Tim never shared anything with me about the issues he was having.

There was an occasion when the four of us—Tim, Lori, Teri and I—went to see *King Lear* at the Stratford Festival. It was desperately hot that day, and in the middle of the production the air conditioning in the theatre broke down. The heat made the room terribly uncomfortable.

At the intermission we decided not to return, instead choosing a local restaurant to have some drinks and dinner. We were all having a good time beating the heat, when all of a sudden the mood changed. I'm not sure what happened, but Lori became angry and insisted that she and Tim head home. I have no idea what set her off, but the pair were soon in their car, leaving Stratford for Toronto. Somewhere on the drive back to their house in Willowdale, Tim got angry, pulled the car over and told her to get out. He then sped off and was a few miles down the road when he realized the stupidity of what he'd done. By the time he returned, Lori was gone, apparently picked up by someone driving by. Both of them arrived home safely, but needless to say, it was a very bitter time.

On another occasion, we were in Toronto at a shopping centre developer/tenant sales meeting and Tim invited us back to his home. Larry Mann, a Canadian actor who had had many roles in Hollywood, was among the group. Lori was out when we arrived at the house, but came home soon afterward. She was livid, though I couldn't figure out why. She grabbed Tim's drink and poured it over his head.

Tim went to make another drink and Lori went off again.

"You touch another drink and I'll break every fucking bottle in this house!" she yelled. It was clear that she might follow through with her threat. With that, Tim left the house, got in his car and left for his friend Ken Gariepy's home, which was nearby. We followed him shortly afterwards.

Soon enough, Lori was calling Ken's house, only to be told that Tim wasn't there. I was hoping the situation would cool down. In the end I called Teri and told her that Lori and Tim had had another argument and I was going to stay until the situation blew over.

The next morning, I had an early meeting. As I left the house, I noticed that my car had four flat tires. Lori had let the air out of Tim's, Ken's and my tires. The situation had gotten ridiculous.

Thankfully, I didn't have to deal with her all that often, though that was soon to change.

ooooo

With his problems at home not improving, and despite my prodding for him to retire and help with Tim Hortons full time, it wasn't all that difficult for Punch Imlach to talk Tim into coming back to play in Buffalo in 1973–74 even though he would turn forty-four during the season. His salary for that season was substantial, but it was structured as a loan so as to defer taxes. As part of the deal, Tim talked Punch into giving him a Pantera sports car.

Though he would be almost completely removed from the business while in Buffalo, I don't think he had any concern about the way I was managing Tim Hortons. "I've got myself a horse," he told his brother when asked about how the business was doing, in reference to me. At the time, all of my focus was on the business. He understood that.

Still, the responsibility of operating TDL, which now had more than thirty stores, could be difficult at times. Without an everyday partner, all of the business's successes and failures were my doing. And not every one of our new stores had been hits. Several had failed to live up to the expectations we had for them, and we were faced with forgiving the royalties and reducing rent charges to these franchise owners just to keep the stores afloat. Unlike other franchise systems, which simply would have resold the stores to other owners, we stuck with the individuals who purchased our stores. They were the guys fighting to keep their businesses running, and it was a twenty-four-hour-a-day job. I felt a lot of empathy for them. After all, it wasn't that much earlier that I had been faced with the same problems. I had been a franchisee, and I felt bad when a franchise struggled.

In some cases, we had no choice but to take back the franchises and run them ourselves in the hope of making them successful. Just as I had a decade earlier, I was still teaching the franchise owners how to bake and helping run the company stores.

On Wednesday, February 20, 1974, Tim was scheduled to play for Buffalo in Toronto, and I planned on heading down to see the game with my wife Teri and Layton Coulter, who managed construction for TDL. We planned to meet after the game at George's Spaghetti House, a restaurant that was frequented by the Toronto Maple Leafs and other players when they were in town, to discuss developing some real estate in Atlantic Canada. At the Buffalo practice the morning before the game, Tim was hit in the jaw by a puck. Despite being in a lot of pain, he was determined to play that night and to meet afterwards.

After the game, the developers, Layton, Teri and I were expecting to meet Tim. He never appeared. After waiting for some time, we decided to go to dinner, figuring he might be there. He never showed up.

We all waited for a while and then drove back to the office in Oakville, where Teri and Layton had left their vehicles. When we arrived at the office, Tim was sitting in the dark, wearing his overcoat and his driving gloves. He had a blue-and-white ice pack on his face, a drink in front of him and his feet on the coffee table. Seeing Tim, I broke into laughter. He looked ridiculous.

"You can laugh, but this really hurts," he said, pushing the ice pack against his face.

We started talking, but after about an hour, Teri and Layton left to go home, leaving Tim and I to talk about our business. It was well past midnight by this point.

We spoke about where we were going with the company. Interestingly, it was the tenth anniversary of the day I had taken over the first Tim

Hortons franchise. But as I filled Tim in on some of the details of the company's plans, including the two new stores in eastern Canada that would be under construction, the tone of the discussion changed. It became a little contentious when I raised the issue of company credit cards. It had bothered me for a while that Tim would use company funds to pay for phone cards used by his family, as well as covering bills at the Donalda Club in Toronto and paying for gas for his family's cars. He had his father named our "Northern Ontario supervisor" and placed on payroll, though we only had three or four stores in the area at the time. It was costing the business a lot of money, which we couldn't afford at the time, but Tim wanted to make everyone around him happy.

"Tim, if we ever get audited, these expenses just won't fly," I told him. "You just can't do this."

"Jeez, Ron, what's the big deal?"

"Well, if you are using the card to entertain your teammates when you are in Los Angeles, it is going to be pretty hard to say it is a business expense," I replied. "How are we going to explain this? This has got to stop or we're going to get nailed."

He got angry at that point, saying he paid his taxes to the government and that this shouldn't be an issue.

"What's the big deal here, Ron? Do you want the whole company to yourself?"

I decided it wasn't worth pursuing and let the matter drop.

By this time I was very tired, and I knew I would have to be in Sarnia early the next morning. And it would take Tim an hour and a half to get back to Buffalo. I suggested it would be easier on him if he spent the night at my place in Burlington. He agreed, said he would lock up, and I got ready to head for home.

"I love you, Blub," he said, referring to me by the nickname he used, and kissing me on the cheek. He had a nickname for most of his friends. Mine was not very flattering, because it was a jibe about my girth. Clearly, from the conclusion of our meeting there were no hard feelings.

It was around 4 a.m. by the time we left, and I was heading along the Queen Elizabeth Way when Tim's Pantera passed me. I fully expected he'd be waiting at my house when I arrived.

ooooo

It has never been quite clear what happened next. By some accounts, Tim was driving the Pantera too fast and missed the exit to head to my home. He certainly had passed me at quite a clip, as I was travelling much faster than I should have in my Lincoln Continental as the QEW had virtually no traffic on it at that hour. Regardless, once he missed my exit, he appeared to have been determined to make it back to his hotel in Buffalo.

When I arrived home and he wasn't there, I went to bed. In my mind, Tim had simply followed a whim and decided it would be better to get home that night.

I was awakened at 6 a.m. by a phone call. I picked up the receiver to find out it was Punch Imlach.

"Ron, I've got some bad news and I want you to call Lori and the kids," he said.

I had just come out of a deep sleep and the call caught me off guard. I wasn't immediately clear about what Punch was saying.

"Tim has been in a car accident."

"How bad is it?" I asked.

"He's dead," he said, with a hint of anger in his voice. "I knew I shouldn't have bought him that fucking car."

With that, he hung up.

8

TIMS ON THE BLOCK

Though Punch Imlach would later say I "forgot" to make the call to the Horton family, that was not the case. The shock from Punch's call left me very upset, and it took a few minutes for me to get my emotions under control. When I called Lori, both phone lines were busy. Given the early hour, I knew that Lori was being informed of Tim's accident. The story made front-page headlines across the country, and Toronto radio station CFRB spent all day talking about his life.

After I determined that the family knew of Tim's death, my next concern was to contact the franchise owners, many of whom would be worried about what Tim's death would mean to their operations. Since Tim was the president, it made sense that some franchise owners had doubts about the future of Tim Hortons. One of the franchise owners called me upon hearing about Tim's accident. He was in shock.

"What are we going to do now? Tim's dead, what's going to happen to us?" he asked. The reality is that very little would change operationally after Tim's death, but we had to get that message out to the franchise owners to make them aware of this fact.

I met with our staff to determine what we should do. We agreed to close the stores the day of the funeral, both in honour of Tim and to allow the store owners and staff to attend. We phoned all the owners we could reach to make them clear about what was happening.

Though Tim died on Thursday morning, Lori made the decision to hold the funeral on Monday so that his Buffalo teammates could attend. Their schedule was such that this was the earliest they could pay respects to their teammate.

After leaving the Oakville offices, George Spicer and I went to the Horton home, and by the time we arrived, a lot of Tim and Lori's friends were there. Lori was very calm. When I expressed my sympathy at the terrible loss we had suffered, her reply caught me off guard.

"Well, Ron, it wasn't a question of how he was going to die, but when."

Tim's four daughters were devastated by his death, but during the days following the accident I never saw Lori shed a tear.

I went to the visitation the next evening at the funeral home. I'll never forget the impact it had on me to see Tim lying in the casket. It was as if I'd been hit over the head with a hammer.

Mel Rothwell—our adviser, friend and partner at Dunwoody & Company—and I drove to St. Catharines soon after to gather his personal effects. It was part of a gentleman's agreement between Tim and me. If either of us died suddenly, the surviving partner would destroy any personal items that might cause embarrassment to the family. We also wanted to see the car and talk with the police. They were very helpful. When we saw the vehicle, many of us speculated that Tim could have survived the crash had he been wearing his seatbelt. He had been thrown from the vehicle on impact, through the passenger door.

The reality was that the address book Tim had on him could have revealed a side of him that few were aware of. Even I had only learned by accident about some of the changes that had occurred during the last year or two of his life. Part of this stems from a company Christmas party in 1973, to which the staff and franchisees were invited. Tim never showed up, though he had been in the Tim Hortons office when I left, and I'd expected him to attend.

Lori called repeatedly, asking for him.

"Ron, do you know where Tim is?" she asked.

I had no idea. At the time, Tim was keeping an apartment in Oakville in order to stay in town if he was needed late at the office. In reality, the apartment was used for other personal matters as well. That evening, I had two parties to attend, with the other being for an investment group that I participated in. As I went to the second party, I thought I'd stop by Tim's apartment and see if he was there. When I found the door open, I simply walked in.

I was quite surprised by what I found. Tim was there with his lovely friend of some time, and they were a happy couple. Apparently they had spoken about making their relationship more permanent, and Tim later told me they planned to leave their respective spouses. I was actually thrilled to hear this. I just wanted to see Tim as happy as he clearly was in this relationship.

ooooo

Years after Tim's death, Lori spent much of her time and money partying. While she was on a trip to Hawaii, which she paid for, with two priests, I called her daughters, Jeri-Lyn, Kim, Kelly and Tracy, and asked them to meet me in Oakville at Tim Donut Ltd. I wanted to impress upon them that their mother's lifestyle could not continue this way. They told me they were well aware of the direction she was headed in, but they had no way of controlling their mom. After lunch at the Omega Restaurant at Kerr Street and Speers Road, Jeri asked if she could speak with me in private. Since we had driven from the office in two cars, I suggested she ride back with me. During the drive, she asked me many questions about her father.

"Before Dad died, was he happy?" she asked, as if to inquire whether he had anyone else in his life.

It was a question I hadn't anticipated, but she had been old enough to recognize that her father's marriage to Lori had been difficult. I thought about the question for a few moments before answering.

"Yes, Jeri-Lyn, he was. He had found someone he was very fond of and I do think they were happy."

"Thanks for telling me that. I'm so glad to hear it."

Lori didn't make a decision about what she would do with the company for several months following Tim's death. She had many things to deal with involving his estate, which kept her busy, but after a period of time Lori determined that she would like to enter the business her husband had helped found. She tried to be involved and would participate in real-estate negotiations and interviews with new franchisees. She seemed to enjoy it at first, but as time passed it seemed more like she was playing a role. It must have been difficult for her, because she'd never been employed outside the home, with the exception of some modelling. She had been a housewife who managed the household and raised four daughters.

The problem was that the company had grown dramatically from its early days in Hamilton, and it would have been difficult for even an experienced businessperson to enter the company. There were now forty-seven stores, with an expansion to Atlantic Canada well under way. We also continued to feel tremendous pressure from our debt, which rendered the success of the chain far from a sure thing. Still, Lori thought she could make it work—at the start, at least.

Another issue was the agreement Tim had drafted, which left the surviving partner with a majority stake in the company.

Tim had said, "Look, Ron, I know you don't want to be partners with my wife, and I sure don't want to be partners with yours, so we should have a shareholder arrangement that deals with that possibility." With that in mind, we had had Ken Gariepy, our mutual friend and lawyer, draft an agreement. The deal was arranged in March 1972, and gave us each ninety-eight common shares, with four shares held in trust by Gariepy. In the event that one of us died, the four shares would be transferred to the surviving partner, giving him clear majority control.

At no time during this period that we worked together did I encourage Lori to become a silent partner. I chose to help her try to find a way for herself in the business. The problem was that Lori didn't bring any value to the partnership. She hadn't been involved at all with the business when Tim was alive, and it was difficult for both of us to have her start learning how to manage such a vibrant operation. She just wasn't suited to business life. In time, her interest in TDL seemed to fade, and she began coming to the office less frequently.

After about a year of managing this way, I concluded that the partnership was not working and we'd have to find a way to change. Lori's personality was just not suited to business negotiations. We couldn't continue on the path we were going, and I felt hamstrung by not having the freedom to make the decisions I would have made without Lori being involved. I became concerned about being too aggressive, fearing that I could put the company in trouble and potentially hurt Lori's financial interests in the process. It caused me to be too careful with decisions, which was not my style. I didn't like to feel restrained from making decisions I thought were necessary; if the status quo were maintained, I felt TDL might never reach its full potential.

In March 1975, Lori and I had lunch at the Country Squire restaurant to discuss the future of the company and all of the concerns I had. It was an open, warm, friendly discussion about what had to be done. In my opinion, there were only three viable options: since the company was named after her late husband, Lori could buy me out; I could try to find a way to buy her out; or we could find a third party to purchase the chain. In hindsight, I suppose a fourth option might have been to take the company public, but at the time I felt these were the three paths we should consider.

It was clear that Lori had absolutely no interest in owning the company herself, but she had no problem if I were to find a way to buy her shares.

"Well, Ron, there's one thing for sure," Lori said. "I am not interested in running this chain. It was your dream and you've built it."

Since I didn't believe I could arrange the needed financing to purchase her shares, we decided to go with the third option and find a willing buyer.

It turned out that there was one company that was particularly keen on buying TDL, and that was Dunkin' Donuts, a U.S.-based chain that had a limited presence in Canada. At the time, it was the most logical company to approach about a sale because they had already made overtures to purchase the chain.

Dunkin' Donuts was the largest donut chain in North America at the time. It had been created in 1950 by William Rosenberg and had grown to become very popular in the States, but it was struggling to gain ground in Canada, though it had become established in Quebec. By the time I entered into discussions with them, William Rosenberg's son, Robert, was the CEO. I was invited down to Massachusetts to discuss potential terms. The company was very keen to move into the Ontario market and recognized that Tim Hortons was gaining brand identification and distribution clout.

I flew to Boston and was met by George Haggerty, one of their vice-presidents and my host. As soon as we arrived at their head office, he was called into an emergency meeting. There was a heated debate in the boardroom that went on for quite a while. Bob Rosenberg finally came and invited me into the meeting with their senior management team. The message was, "We can't go forward with a deal."

It turns out that thirteen franchise owners in Philadelphia had previously launched a class-action lawsuit against the company for wrongful profits and were seeking compensation of $80 million. A ruling against Dunkin' Donuts could put the company in a precarious position. That decision had been handed down on the morning of my arrival. The judge found 100 percent in favour of the franchisees, and the ruling effectively meant that Dunkin' Donuts was history if the company could not get the judgment overturned. Bob told me years later that, after hearing the news, he left the office, went home and was sick to his stomach.

The failure of the deal with Dunkin' Donuts was a disappointing blow to me at the time, and one of several problems I faced. There was no way I could take the business forward with Lori as a partner, but I wasn't sure that there was any way I could come up with the money to acquire the company outright. On top of this, upon returning from Boston, I discovered that Teri had decided to leave with our children. She left no forwarding address or phone number where they could be reached.

My lifestyle, with its endless business trips, had been hard on Teri. She wanted the benefits that came with a strong work ethic, but I always felt she wasn't willing to put up with the sacrifices I needed to make to obtain them. She was never happy with the fact that I was still working long hours and travelling across Canada doing site work and store supervision because we had very few people in that capacity. Of course, we managed to occasionally find time for holidays, but they were infrequent. I can't claim the marriage was a mistake, since we have three wonderful children from it, but in hindsight it was clearly never meant to be successful. Near the end of our marriage, things became very difficult. In the final years of our marriage, I just wanted to keep things together for the children, but I knew that would prove difficult. If she had not taken it upon herself to leave, I would never have ended the marriage. However, I certainly must share the blame for our divorce. The dissolution of our marriage can not be blamed on Teri; certainly the countless days I was away from home on business were difficult for her and I was never the easiest person to be married to.

The breakup of my marriage wasn't the only problem I faced during that period. One morning while negotiating the sale with Lori, I walked to my car, which was parked in the lot of our office on Sinclair Road. The next thing I knew, I was flat on my back on the hood of my car. I had passed out.

Concerned that this might be a serious medical condition, I went to see my doctor. I was told that my schedule and the stress I was under had led to the blackout. He put me on medication and indicated that I would have to slow down.

Today, when I look back at that time, I wonder how I survived all the turmoil. But I always performed well under some degree of stress, and I needed very little sleep to be able to put in extremely long days. I was regularly exhausted, but a few hours of sleep would allow me to get right back to work. I recognized that my work ethic, which had remained from the days when I had to work several jobs in the early 1960s, had become my strength. I had just turned forty-five, and the long work days didn't promise to end any time soon.

One thing I did take from this episode was to seriously consider my options with Tim Hortons. Not only was I not sure whether I could raise the capital to buy the company outright, but I didn't even know the true value of TDL. The company's financial adviser, Mel Rothwell, a personal friend of both Lori and me, was asked to help determine a fair price. Mel had been a friend of Maple Leafs forward Dave Keon and was recommended to Tim and me in 1968.

Mel agreed to do a valuation of the company, but noted that we would also need a second independent appraisal. He recommended Price Waterhouse. Mel priced the company at about $1.5 million, meaning our stakes were worth $750,000 apiece. Ron Anson-Cartwright of Price Waterhouse determined the company was worth more. The agreed-upon price that Price Waterhouse came up with was $1.7 million, or $850,000 each, which became the amount I would need to purchase Lori's shares. On May 5, 1975, I made Lori an offer of $200,000 as a cash down payment, with the remainder to be paid in five annual instalments. This offer was rejected. I would have to come up with the full amount as a lump sum.

For most of our partnership, I had been pretty much left to my own devices when it came to raising money for the operation. I had to convince people of the viability of the chain and my ability to manage it. Thanks to my passion for the business, we were always able to obtain financing, but often on unfavourable terms. This was true even now, ten years into the venture. And it would represent an added burden for me to borrow such a large amount of capital to purchase Lori's shares.

However, as a chain that boasted forty-eight restaurants with strong cash flows, Tim Hortons was starting to get noticed in some established financial circles. Alan Pyle, who was with the Mercantile Bank of Canada, a division of Citicorp, had heard about my difficulties in obtaining financing. Mercantile had a more aggressive mentality than its Canadian counterparts, and it was actively seeking businesses to which it could extend credit. This was a stark contrast to the attitudes of the Canadian financial institutions, which avoided becoming involved in business ventures that showed any degree of risk. Alan observed that, although the company's debt load was significant, the chain's growth would be a sufficient guarantee for him to offer me the loan I needed to acquire Lori's half of the business. As part of the arrangement, Mercantile would receive all of the shares and personal guarantees in the company to hold in trust.

When I received the approval from the Mercantile Bank, Lori and I met with our respective lawyers to finalize the transaction. But it turned out that the transaction wasn't going to be as simple as one might have expected. Jim Blaney, a partner in the prominent Toronto law firm of Blaney, Pasternak, represented Lori during the negotiation. Jim indicated at the meeting that the amount to purchase Lori's shares had changed.

Blaney met us with the news that Lori now wanted $1 million for her stake. I was stunned. I'd expected to simply sign the papers and get on with things, but once more a stumbling block had appeared. Since I had already promised all of the company's shares to Mercantile Bank in exchange for $850,000, I wasn't prepared to come up with another

$150,000. I was upset with both Lori and Blaney because we had already negotiated and agreed upon the price. Now I was being told I had two weeks to come up with the additional money. I think there was some thought that I couldn't come up with the rest of the money; to this day I wonder what would have happened had I told them I couldn't. Without any options, Lori might have had to accept the $850,000.

I was seriously concerned that the deal might fall apart, so I approached my brother-in-law, Gord Oliver, who was a branch manager for the Toronto-Dominion Bank. He had been trying, unsuccessfully, to help raise the money to acquire the company from Lori. When this latest hurdle popped up, Gord said he could help me with an additional $100,000. That still left me scrambling for the balance, which I took out of the company's working capital.

The deal was finally signed on Tuesday, December 23, 1975. There was one last problem: we arrived early in the morning, and it became apparent that my lawyer hadn't really been capable of overseeing this sort of transaction. It turned out it was simply too large for him, and most of his paperwork was out of order and had to be redone. Alan Pyle, who came to the closing with us, was sick with the flu and had to struggle along as all of the official documents for the closing were redone. He suggested that my lawyer was not very competent.

As soon as the deal was finalized, Alan took the shares for the company from me and pushed a cheque for $850,000 across the table towards me. In turn, I gave Lori a cheque, by far the largest cheque I had ever written.

"Lori, this money should be drawing interest for you over the weekend, so we should go and deposit it soon," I told her, noting that the banks would be soon be closed for the afternoon—and the Christmas holidays. We would have to hurry if Lori was to get the money deposited. We went to a nearby branch of the Toronto-Dominion Bank in downtown Toronto, approached the teller and told her we wanted to deposit a handwritten cheque for $1 million. The teller looked perplexed.

"I can't accept a personal cheque for that amount," she told us.

"Please call the branch manager of the Toronto-Dominion Bank at Aberdeen and Dundurn in Hamilton. He'll approve the transaction," I explained.

Once the phone call was made, the teller was given a clearance number and was told to accept the cheque. It was placed in an interest-bearing account for the weekend.

I still remember how happy Lori looked as everything came to a close. We had finished our business dealings and remained friends. She was a rich woman with $1 million in her bank account and I was very much in debt, owing more than half the market value of the chain.

Lori wanted out of the business, but she had little to keep her occupied other than the Tim Horton Memorial Camp, near Parry Sound in Ontario's Muskoka region, which was built to honour Tim. Long after she had sold her shares, I continued to invite her along to open new stores with me. It gave her something to do, and the people at the stores always enjoyed meeting her and hearing stories about Tim. She also continued to travel with me, right through to the opening of the sixty-fifth store in Dartmouth—the last store I actually baked in. We remained friends for many years. Unfortunately, neither our friendship nor her money would last.

9

TIMBIT AFTERMATH

Buying Lori's stake in TDL allowed me to move forward. Borrowing the capital through Alan Pyle at the Mercantile Bank of Canada also meant that the bank had a keen interest in the success and progress of Tim Hortons. A few months after the deal closed, Alan approached me with a proposal.

"Ron, I think you have a great business here, and I think you can make it work," he said. He proceeded to say that Mercantile was willing to make additional financing available so that Tim Hortons could expand.

"I think we can offer you a line of credit for the capital required for further expansion. We don't want to fund you one store at a time, but rather several stores that would be approved for advancement of $1 million," he told me. The limitation was based on our monthly updates and annual statements that showed what appeared to be a fantastic growth opportunity. The interest rate on the financing would be prime plus one percent. This would cause us a lot of discomfort in the early 1980s, when interest rates shot up to 22 percent—tough enough for a company that was still very capital-intensive, and especially so at a time when new stores in Quebec and western Canada were underperforming.

Mercantile's continued confidence—and interest—in the success of Tim Hortons was the catalyst that allowed us to bring the company into new markets. By the late 1970s, Tim Hortons was well established in Ontario with a few stores in Atlantic Canada. The additional funds would allow us to make Tim Hortons a truly national chain. We started looking for opportunities across the country, and were pleasantly surprised to find that there were a number that eagerly presented themselves. Canada was embracing the company in a way that we had not foreseen a decade earlier.

Even with Mercantile's infusion of capital, we still made affordability the number one determining factor in selecting our locations. We strove to find sites where we could own 50 percent of the real estate, and at the very least we made sure we controlled the leases of all the properties on which we had stores. This enabled us to increase our cash flow, but proved to be a costly undertaking.

While we couldn't necessarily afford the best locations, we worked hard to acquire firm secondary sites, which typically cost around $40,000 during the early 1970s. Taking into account the costs of purchasing or leasing the land, building the restaurant and purchasing the equipment, it could cost us $150,000 to open a store. By comparison, in some instances it can cost more than $1 million to build and open a new store today. But as people became more familiar with the Tim Hortons brand, investors started approaching TDL about placing stores in their developments. They knew that Tim Hortons generated customer traffic that would benefit their other tenants.

In 1976, TDL continued its expansion into Atlantic Canada, where sales had surged. Gary O'Neill, who owned our successful first store in Moncton, indicated to us that he would like to own a second franchise there. However, money was still tight for Gary. "Gary, you could barely afford to open the first store," I told him. "How can you possibly afford two?" He assured me he was willing to pay cash, and while I have no idea where he managed to find the money, he did open the second store, and it turned out to be another success for him and the chain. As had been the case with the early stores in Hamilton, opening several stores within a specific area like Moncton generally had a synergistic effect on the established outlets. Sales at these stores might dip in the short term, but over a few years the additional locations would strengthen the brand, and traffic patterns and population distribution would change, which generated additional business for all. A place like Moncton would eventually be home to more than thirty stores, the largest number per capita in Canada.

Sometimes, unexpected opportunities arose when we were out scouting new store locations. One such incident occurred in 1976, when I went to Prince Edward Island in search of a location for a store in Charlottetown. It didn't take long to find the right spot—a house sitting right next to a McDonald's—on a busy business strip. The house was almost entirely surrounded by the McDonald's parking lot. I went up to the door of the house and was greeted by the tenants, who told me they thought the home might be for sale and that I should contact the owner, a woman named Mrs. Verna Kent, in Halifax.

I called the number and introduced myself to her.

"Mrs. Kent, I represent the Tim Hortons Donuts chain and hoped I might speak to you about whether your house in Charlottetown is for sale."

"Indeed it is, Mr. Joyce, but there's been a death in my family and I can't possibly speak to you about this matter now," she said in a formal tone. "However, if you give me your number, I'll call you back in due course."

Sure enough, she called me back about the house. It was for sale, she said, and told me the price. I agreed it was a fair price and told her I'd be willing to acquire the property.

"Well, Mr. Joyce, I'd be pleased to sell you the house, but I must tell you I have an agreement with the owner of the McDonald's that I'd give him the right of first refusal," she said. "But I'll present him with your offer price and see if he's willing to match it."

I told her that would be fine, but asked her not to mention I was with Tim Hortons when she spoke with the owner of the McDonald's. Soon afterwards she called the owner, a Mr. Johnson, and informed him that he could buy the property at our agreed-upon price, and that he had ten minutes to make up his mind. He declined. I guess he thought she was bluffing.

Mrs. Kent called me soon after.

"Mr. Joyce, you've bought yourself a property," she said. It was a fascinating deal, in that it had all been done over the phone. There wasn't even a handshake to seal the arrangement.

Of course, when word spread that TDL had purchased the land for a Tim Hortons restaurant, the owner of the McDonald's offered Mrs. Kent more money than the price she had agreed to with me. To her credit, she stuck by her word and the deal, though there was no paperwork signed and she was being pressured by others to back out. At the closing in Halifax, Mrs. Kent's lawyer was concerned that she could have received more than we were paying. Her concern, meanwhile, was that I would resell the house to Mr. Johnson at a profit. I indicated to her that this would not be the case, but that if I did sell the property, any excess would go to her benefit. We then finished the deal and maintained a friendship that lasted many years, and in fact, we still communicate to this day.

The success of our new restaurants also presented opportunities that we didn't anticipate at first. For example, we entered into negotiations for two sites in Burlington, Ontario, that were very close together—one on Appleby Line and the other on Fairview Street. When the city's zoning department approved both locations, we had to choose which one we should develop and which one to sell. But after we discussed the sites with the prospective owners, Eldon and Doreen Fawcett, we decided to proceed with restaurants on *both* sites. The Fawcetts purchased both franchises, and the stores opened just days apart. Both were successful right out of the gate, without hurting sales at existing locations. Later, we would lease another successful location that was directly across the road from the Appleby Line store. The rationale was that each store had its own unique traffic pattern, and even though they were right across the street from one another, they would attract different customers.

ooooo

As we became established in Atlantic Canada, the notion of moving into Quebec became a pressing issue for the company. For a while, TDL was being courted by Quebec businessmen who wanted to acquire a master franchise. A master licence meant that one individual would represent the company and sell franchises within a specific area—in this case, Quebec. It would have removed some of the costs associated with finding and selling franchises, but it would also have lessened the control that TDL had over franchises in the province and lowered the fees head office collected from store owners. It was a concept that TDL never bought into. For other franchisors, selling master licences was a short-term solution that led to long-term problems and a lack of control over their own brand.

Henry Svazas, our real-estate acquisition manager, was not initially interested in moving into Quebec when the idea presented itself again. Indeed, an important consideration was the presence of Dunkin' Donuts, which was well established with more than 100 stores in the province by the time we opened our first, in Rosemère (about half an hour north of Montreal), on July 23, 1977. Quebec was Dunkin' Donuts' best market in all of North America and we were somewhat concerned whether we could maintain a foothold there.

However, it didn't take long before renegade franchise operators at Dunkin' Donuts felt they understood their market better than their parent company and started offering products that deviated from what was being sold in the rest of the chain. Some stores were serving bacon and eggs in the morning as well as the donuts that were the chain's staple. These issues began to hurt the chain as more Dunkin' Donuts stores started offering their own variations on the company's menu.

Even though Dunkin' Donuts appeared to be vulnerable, and despite my initial confidence that we could successfully bring the brand into Quebec, we struggled to become successful in the province. We had followed a similar strategy to the one we'd initially employed in Ontario, opening in smaller markets like Rosemère. Three years later, in 1980, we opened additional stores in Boucherville and Sept-Îles. However, it took longer than expected to reach our goals. It wasn't until the quality of Dunkin' Donuts' operations diminished a few years later, and the American donut chain began closing stores, that Tim Hortons made a true breakthrough in Quebec.

As the Tim Hortons name spread, it became apparent that providing a consistent experience across all of our restaurants would prove difficult. If some store owners weren't offering the best donuts and coffee, or failed to keep their restrooms or parking lots clean, it reflected not only on that store, but on the entire chain. In the franchise system, if half of your stores fail to live up to the standards set out for the chain, the company will likely fail. The aim of any franchise operation should be to have 100 percent of its stores living up to the company's expectations. Of course, we realized that this was an unrealistic goal, so our target was a minimum of 95 percent of stores that met our standards.

To ensure that our store owners were maintaining their operations to our satisfaction, we would regularly make unannounced visits to the stores. We found that, even before we walked in the front door, it was possible to distinguish a good operation from one that was lacking—some shortfalls were just that obvious. Upon driving onto the property, we would take a look at the parking lot. Was it clean? Had the garbage cans been emptied recently, or were they overflowing? Then, upon entering the store, one of the first things we paid attention to was the ambience. In a good operation, the store would be clean and our food would be fresh and baked appropriately.

In some instances, this was not the case. Since we had such high standards for the quality and freshness of our food, discussions with store owners would occasionally result in confrontations over our expectations. I recall one franchisee who felt he was being unfairly chastised for the state of his restaurant.

"Ron, what do you expect from us?" he asked after I had pointed out some deficiencies in his operation. "This is good enough," he protested. But "good enough" was not a standard I wanted my owners to aim for. If the company was to become the leader in the food-service industry, we had to be better than all of our competition. It was never "good enough"—there was always better.

These visits weren't meant as a means of controlling the owners or catching them out. They knew exactly what I expected of them, especially over the first decade of the chain, when many of them were trained by me personally. The philosophy of Tim Hortons was clear: freshness was expected in everything we did. Some of the store owners probably felt my appearances in the stores were staged, but there was no play-acting involved. My passion for the business was real. Often, the stores would be completely transformed after these visits. And some of the franchisees I was hardest on went on to become the most successful.

Though we could be hard on franchisees that deviated from our standards, the company also had a very responsible attitude towards our store owners. It was something that set TDL apart from other franchise operators. If a store opened and didn't meet financial targets, we would come to the store and work with the store owners for however long it took to resolve any problems with their operation. In some locations, we would even subsidize it and forgive royalties in order to keep it operating. It was a strategy designed to make the overall company stronger, and it meant we rarely closed any restaurants. Other franchises would use a similar strategy, but unlike Tim Hortons, they never forgave royalties. That meant that, even if a store survived, the owner would spend years paying back royalties from the fallow period.

In order to adhere to the standards we expected, the company had to address the way we trained new store operators. Training was something I played a large role in, but after the first decade it was becoming ever more difficult for me to find the time to dedicate to it. Up until 1976, when new owners would start one of our franchises, we would send them to another store, where they would attempt to learn all of the business's facets before setting foot in their own operation.

It was not a satisfactory way of training, because the process kept us from having a consistent standard across the chain. Deviations between stores would creep in, depending on whom the owner had trained with. Though the new owners would typically learn from some of the best store owners, this method of training meant that there was a wide variety of acceptable standards. The training was also almost exclusively practical—there was little theory on how to run a business, something that would have helped many of our operators who were managing a business for the first time.

The answer to these issues was what would become known as "Donut University." Despite its grand title, Donut University was really a training centre in the basement of a store in Hamilton. It was TDL's attempt to make the company more professional by providing standardized training, and although it was not nearly as sophisticated as it would later become, it provided a solid foundation from which to work.

The classroom was located directly below the store, which allowed us to teach the new owners and have them test out what they learned upstairs. Compared to the training we had undertaken to that point, the new program was far more intensive. In four weeks, new owners had to learn every aspect of running a Tim Hortons and be able to run a shift themselves. Since some owners had difficulty coping with the fast pace of their stores once they opened, Donut University was a great way for them to gain an understanding of what they could expect.

At the same time we were investing in the business's expansion, we were also investigating new ways to expand our product line. In order to succeed, a company has to continually innovate. To many outside observers, Tim Hortons may have appeared to be successful in everything the company had attempted. In fact, the company's success was built on testing and trying new products; often, ideas failed to live up to their potential or our expectations. Although it may seem counterintuitive, making mistakes in business can actually be a good thing. If you don't make mistakes, it typically means you aren't taking enough risks that will lead to continued success. Some ideas will work and some won't. A culture of innovation in a business comes hand in hand with a tolerance of failure.

Few will recall many of the unsuccessful attempts to expand our menu beyond coffee and donuts, but they began early in the company's history. One product the chain introduced was ice cream. Tim personally loved ice cream and insisted that we sell it in some of our first stores. Being a seasonal item, it created all sorts of staffing problems, and since the earliest stores operated with very few employees, the ice cream would take their focus away from our main products.

At this same time, we decided to introduce pies in our stores. Pies seemed like a natural fit for Tim Hortons, as they were baked products that our customers could purchase at the store and take home to enjoy. Also, we had recently begun making croissants, so the necessary ovens were installed in some of the stores. I went to California to see a chain called Marie Callendar, which specialized in pies and had developed a strong following. On one of my visits, I met Don Callendar, the man behind the chain, and explained to him what TDL was trying to do. Sensing that Tim Hortons wasn't going to be competition for his U.S. stores, he toured me through his operation and provided me with a sense of what it would take to successfully sell pies. Like many new product launches, the pies only found a niche in the market for a short time. They also proved very labour-intensive and costly, and quality control between our various stores was difficult to maintain.

It wasn't long, however, before the company added another staple to our menu. In 1975, we introduced small, round donuts that looked like the centre scraps from our donuts. In fact, these "donut holes" were created and baked specifically, and they took a fair bit of effort to create. We didn't find much success with them initially, but Burlington franchise owners Eldon and Doreen Fawcett had done reasonably well selling them in their stores. The concept appeared to be a bit of a fad, and in time customers at the store seemed to lose interest. In 1976, after some deliberation, we decided to revisit this idea across the chain. We felt that with the right branding, the donut hole could become a successful complement to our existing offerings. We knew it would need to have a significant marketing push behind it in order to catch on, so we planned to launch the most important advertising campaign in the company's history to support it.

Given its contemporary reputation as a leader in marketing, it surprises people to know how little promotion and advertising Tim Hortons did in its early years. Though there was supposedly a budget set aside for "promotions" as far back as our first store, the truth is that little was done in the company's early years. Tim had taken out an advertisement in the *Hamilton Spectator* in 1964, but by the time the Ottawa Street store was through its third operator in less than a year, there was no money left to promote the business.

We had done a few radio spots in the following years, purchasing inexpensive air time on a local station. But these spots made little impact. We continued to do some occasional advertising, largely because the franchises paid a percentage of their sales towards a promotions budget. In the early 1970s, Tim Donut Ltd. did some regional television spots, commercials that featured Tim with athletes like the Toronto Maple Leafs' George Armstrong and Pat Quinn, as well as the Hamilton Tiger-Cats' Gary Inskeep and Angelo Mosca, who later became a professional wrestler. The commercial that features all five was shot at the seventeenth Tim Hortons store, located on Trafalgar Road in Oakville, which was company-owned and contained a small training store. We closed the store to shoot the commercial, and the theme behind the spot was "You meet the nicest people at Tim Hortons." The five celebrities were sitting on stools at the serving counter, and the first in line was the burly Mosca. Being the character he was, in rehearsal he had taken a chocolate éclair and smeared whipped cream and chocolate on his face. When the cameras rolled, everyone in the group followed Mosca's lead, and as the camera panned the line of athletes, it revealed their chocolate-and-whipped-cream-covered faces. We decided to use this footage in the final cut of the commercial. After the shoot, we went to our office on Sinclair Road for a few drinks. As a means of thanking the four athletes for their time, Tim presented them with an honorarium.

But George Armstrong would have none of it.

"You're not going to take any money from my buddy," Armstrong said, tearing up all five cheques.

Our stars were putting back Rusty Nails and looked to be in poor shape by the time Mosca and Inskeep left for a Ti-Cats practice at Ivor Wynne, while the rest of us grabbed cabs to our various homes much later on.

Though the commercial went over well, we decided to forego advertising and make our store operations themselves the main marketing tool. We drove home the point to the store owners that they would prosper if they put more energy into their operations. The aim was to have customers become so pleased with the service and products we offered that they would talk about it with their friends. Given our regional approach and the fact that many of our stores were in smaller towns and cities in Ontario, this grassroots appeal proved very successful.

However, the plan for the launch of our new item required a broader mass-market promotion. We hired an advertising agency to help coordinate the marketing, but we still faced a significant hurdle: the new donut had not been named.

We wanted something distinctive that would immediately resonate in the minds of our customers. Something that was representative, but catchy.

One evening, the management team was in the boardroom, brainstorming, when Layton Coulter, our construction coordinator, said something that caught our attention.

"It is really just a tidbit," he said, and we knew immediately what we'd call the product: Timbits. It was perfect. Of course, no one would know what a Timbit was, so we started a campaign designed to get people thinking about the name. "Timbits are coming," we announced. It immediately caught the attention of our customers, and the Timbit was a massive success once it debuted in stores. Customers fell in love with them, which probably had something to do with their size, and the fact they came in eighteen varieties. Maybe our customers felt that by eating Timbits, they were cutting back from eating donuts. In reality, though, they would often consume six or seven Timbits, so they really weren't changing their eating habits at all.

ooooo

Despite the success of the Timbits campaign, marketing always seemed to be a problem for the company. In our early years, it was always hard to gauge the success of our advertisements. Without question, awareness of the Tim Hortons brand grew, but it was never clear that advertising put dollars in our cash registers or added to the bottom line. My mixed feelings on mass advertising led Tim Hortons to concentrate on point-of-purchase marketing.

An alternative product idea serves as an example. When I went into a bakery on Mountain Road in Burlington, I was struck by their strawberry tarts, which were remarkably good. These tarts were stacked full of strawberries, and I purchased half a dozen and took them to the office. I thought the tarts could complement our existing menu.

We baked our own tarts, which we called "Tim Tarts." They were introduced with a marketing campaign that included radio and television commercials. The customers loved them, and we had difficulty keeping stores supplied with strawberries and pastry cups. Although the tarts were not very popular with store owners (they proved to be quite labour-intensive), it became an annual marketing event and a success story. The promotion of the Tim Tart created huge awareness of the variety of products we carried in the stores. We also created special carry-out boxes adorned with colourful strawberries and graphics. Point-of-purchase packaging, like the Timbit and Tim Tart boxes and hot and cold drink cups, became mainstays in our stores from that point onward. The point-of-purchase advertising and promotions garnered a lot of customer attention and were relatively inexpensive. The only drawback: they needed changing very regularly, or customers would fail to notice them. A new in-store advertisement would only stay in the consumer's consciousness for a few weeks before it faded into the background. So, we started rotating our in-store promotions every couple of weeks.

Another product introduction that has since disappeared was our successful cake program, which for a time increased our sales greatly. We created refrigerated showcases to display the beautifully decorated cakes, as it was important to have them visible to the customer. They soon became popular for birthdays, anniversaries and other special occasions. Stores that embraced the concept and spent time decorating and finishing them experienced high-volume sales. One store owner from Owen Sound, Fay Harshman, was a leader in sales and in encouraging other owners as to how to make their cake programs successful. Fay enjoyed sales of $100,000 plus per annum, and many other store owners did very well, too. However, like many of our other products, the cakes disappeared in recent years as the company's product focus changed.

Eventually, we decided to create our own registered advertising agency so that we could avoid paying the mark-up of an outside agency. The approach was not dissimilar to the one we used to create the distribution centre, which allowed us to avoid a middleman and receive volume discounts. After all, it did not make sense to pay someone else a premium to place and create advertisements for Tim Hortons when we could do it ourselves. It turned out to be very successful. Like the franchise fee paid by the company's store owners, our advertising royalty was very slight at the start. As the chain experienced rapid success, we increased the advertising fund's percentage of gross sales to 4 percent. One-half of one percent was to be used in local marketing by the store owners. That led to increased advertising and our foray into more prominent television advertising.

∞∞∞

Though the company had been in business for more than a decade, our customers still primarily visited the chain during the morning. In an attempt to generate more lunchtime traffic, we came up with the concept of Tim Hortons Breakaway in 1977, in conjunction with the opening of our new training centre on Main Street in Hamilton. We developed a separate area with its own signage, entrance, baking equipment and counter, and attempted to create a separate brand with limited hours that sold mainly soup and sandwiches.

We struggled with the Breakaway concept for a number of years, opening a total of nine stores in a variety of locations. Setting up the stores as separate operations from Tim Hortons proved to be their undoing. In retrospect, it is clear that we should have kept the new operation as part of the core restaurant chain. By promoting it under its own name, it meant we had to market it separately from Tim Hortons, which was very costly and largely unsuccessful. The additional employees needed to staff the separate stores also drove up labour costs. Eventually it became clear the concept was failing and would not be our entree into the lunch market so we closed the Breakaway parts of the stores.

However, we remained undaunted by the Breakaway failure and, confident after the success of the Timbit, we continued looking for additions to our traditional menu.

In the mid-1980s, cinnamon buns became very popular and stores sprung up to sell them, even exhausting the smell of cinnamon buns into malls. This product appeared on our radar screen early on, as stores that sold buns were quickly gaining a foothold in the U.S., specifically the TJ Cinnamons chain, which originated in Kansas City.

During this period, the senior management of TDL was scheduled to attend a regional meeting in Brockville, Ontario. Our plane was fuelled and ready to take off when we received word that Brockville was fogged in.

"It is zero-zero, right to the ground in Brockville," the pilot told us. "There's no way you can land there today."

Realizing it would take several hours to drive from Oakville to Brockville, we allowed our operations team to conduct the meeting rather than cancel. Then, the pilot was instructed to take the aircraft to Kansas City. We decided we were going in search of the latest food craze.

On our arrival in Kansas City, we visited two TJ Cinnamons stores. The TDL management team scoured the stores, asking questions and looking at the operation. It was clear from the amount of business they were doing that this was the hottest food concept to appear for some time.

Upon returning to Canada, we became determined to begin selling them within a few months. In retrospect, I realize the concept of cinnamon buns was forced on store owners, many of whom felt that creating the product was too labour-intensive. It turned out the franchise owners were right; cinnamon buns were too hard to make while maintaining the appropriate quality. But the concept would not go away. Recently, Tim Hortons reintroduced cinnamon buns, and because they are shipped frozen, the quality is more consistent.

Though some of our attempts to bring new products to our stores were not successful, bringing new foods into Tim Hortons was one of the reasons the chain remained successful. You always have to keep a business evolving. It can be a subtle change, but it has to be a change for the better. Tim Hortons had started as a small donut shop on Ottawa Street in Hamilton and was on the way to becoming a major restaurant chain in all of Canada. But that was accomplished by changing the stores and the mix of products over time.

One of the most significant changes in the company's history was brought on by a decision to revisit ways of bringing customers into the stores after our morning rush. Though the Breakaway concept had failed, we continued to consciously look at how we might build our lunch business. That led to the creation of our soup and sandwich program, which began in 1985.

Interestingly, TDL cannot take full credit for the concept that would eventually drive our lunch business. It was Dunkin' Donuts, specifically in the Quebec market, that had developed the idea of serving soup in its stores as a means of offsetting its typical morning traffic flow. We were not offering soup when TDL started opening stores in Quebec. Realizing that we were having trouble competing with Dunkin' Donuts, we followed their lead. We were so successful in Quebec that we took the concept into other markets, where we also witnessed a favourable response.

In a similar fashion, introducing sandwiches into our stores was an evolutionary process. The sandwich program began with croissants, which were a big hit when they were first introduced in 1983. Eventually, some stores deviated from the menu and started making croissant sandwiches in several locations in British Columbia. Though we discouraged our franchisees from offering products that were not standard in all of our stores, the croissant sandwiches proved to be quite successful, and we created a standard menu across the chain. This was the beginning of our sandwich program.

Unfortunately, the official launch of our lunch program in 1985 was a huge disappointment. The philosophy of Tim Hortons was clear to all involved: everything must be fresh. But heedless of that fact, the marketing and operations department at TDL determined that the most effective way to introduce sandwiches would be to make them at night and then wrap them in plastic. Cost efficiencies and the store owners' labour concerns were placed ahead of our prime directive.

Soon after the sandwich campaign launched, I ventured into one of the stores. The sandwiches were wrapped, but it was clear they were

Life in Tatamagouche. I'm at the back left, beside my mother, Grace, and my brother, Willard, who's standing next to my sister, Gwen. This marvellous woman raised the three of us on her own, having become a widow at 23 years of age.

Hamilton seemed like a big city when I arrived in 1946. Unlike in Tatamagouche, it was easy to find work. I worked in several factories in my first few years there and made more money than I had ever expected. Also in this photo is Ed Mattatall, my good friend who would later buy one of the first Tim Hortons franchises from me.

I joined the Canadian Navy in 1951, and would remain in active service for five years and as a reserve for another eight years.

Walking the beat. Working as a police officer was not always the most interesting job. I didn't make a great salary, and soon looked into other options, including the restaurant business.

With Tim outside store number four in Hamilton in 1967 as Tim was in the midst of negotiating his contract. Despite a shaky start, I became close friends with him in our eight years as business partners.

Tim Horton in our Oakville warehouse in 1971. Though hockey kept Tim busy for much of the year, he still tried to remain active in the business.

With the chain rapidly expanding, we decided to establish a professional training centre, which became known as "Donut University," in the basement of a store in Hamilton in February 1977. Hamilton Mayor Jack MacDonald (top) carries out several boxes of donuts at our grand opening. The other photo shows how the interior of our stores looked at the time.

In order to buy Lori Horton's stake in TDL, I borrowed most of the money I needed from the Mercantile Bank of Canada. It took me many years to pay the loan off. Here I am, after we repaid the loan in 1983, with Alan Pyle (to my left), the man who agreed to finance the purchase. My financial adviser, Mel Rothwell (far right) and Bert Davidson, chair of the Mercantile Bank of Canada, look on.

The creation of the Tim Horton Children's Foundation has been a labour of love for me over the past three decades. The logo, pictured here, represents Tim's arms protecting a child.

Standing alongside Colin Millar, the Hamilton police chief and my former partner on the force, at the announcement of our bid to bring an NHL team to town. Our offer was the only one that was fully financed, but it was still turned down.

Though she would say otherwise in later years, I always got along well with Tim's widow, Lori. She often traveled with me to store openings even after she sold her stake in the business. Gary O'Neill, the first store owner in Atlantic Canada, is on the left in this photo taken in 1980.

We advertised little in the early years, but we did manage to gather Tim, Hamilton Tiger Cats' stars Angelo Mosca (middle), and Gary Inskeep (far left), as well as Maple Leafs George Armstrong (beside Tim) and Pat Quinn (second from left) for a rare TV commercial.

Speaking at an owners meeting in the late 1970s. I always believed that I worked for the store owners. Notice the Tim Mug, one of the first coffee holders, sitting on the podium.

The employees and owners are key to the chain's ongoing success. As we expanded in the 1980s and '90s, we offered existing Tim Hortons owners more franchises. I wanted every one of them to be successful.

not the fresh products that we had promised our customers. It was a breakdown in the fundamentals that had made Tim Hortons so successful. And without fresh products, Tim Hortons would not have been able to differentiate itself from what could be purchased in corner stores and gas bars. The sandwich program was already under way chainwide when the problem was discovered; rather than go ahead with sandwiches that didn't fit my vision for the chain, we scrapped the idea and went back to trying to find a way to offer them fresh to the customer.

The change in the launch angered a lot of the franchise owners, who were concerned that making fresh sandwiches would increase costs. However, the fresh-to-order menu, which is still used in the chain's restaurants, was so successful that these concerns were eventually forgotten.

The failure of the initial sandwich program demonstrated the difference between entrepreneurs and more traditional management with an expertise in running a company's operations. Those executives who are focused on operations tend to look for the most efficient way to offer a product, while entrepreneurs have to look inside the mind of the consumer and understand how to please them. Often, these two management styles fail to find common ground on how to promote a business.

Of course, of all the products developed by the company, Tim Hortons' coffee has been the most popular. When I acquired the first franchise, a coffee and a donut cost a dime each at the counter. A carry-out box of a dozen donuts cost 69 cents. The prices stayed constant for most of the 1960s, and then rose to 15 cents, or 50 percent. We apologized to our customers for the increase, but it was absolutely necessary since the price of coffee beans, supplies and operations had also risen. Typically, price increases were done in five-cent increments, and we made it a policy to post notices to alert the customers in advance—thereby, we hoped, reducing friction.

Initially, we ground all of our coffee at the front counters; the aroma of freshly ground beans created an aroma that, we felt, stimulated sales. It was standard practice in donut shops south of the border, and something we implemented in our first twelve to fifteen stores. We purchased roasted beans from our supplier, Mother Parkers, and they were ground in Hobart grinders. The goal was a consistent throw of 2.5 ounces of fresh coffee, but even one bad bean could cause the resulting pot of coffee to taste rancid. Achieving consistency was often a significant problem. I came to the conclusion that grinding the beans in the stores had to stop, and I worked with Mother Parkers to develop and grind a blend that would be shipped to us in pre-measured, 2.5-ounce vacuum-sealed packages, thus ensuring freshness and consistency across the chain. This change in direction was the greatest thing we did in establishing quality control and freshness for our consumers. Mother Parkers still supplies coffee to Tim Hortons today, along with other firms including Nestlé, General Foods and TDL, all of whom have duplicated the taste and quality that have remained constant some forty years later.

The taste of Tim Hortons' coffee was actually quite calculated. In the early days, we knew what kind of blend we wanted—largely a middle-of-the-road flavour that would not be too strong or off-putting. Since the early days, we have always served 18-percent cream, as opposed to the 10-percent or "half and half" that is standard elsewhere, and this has been a draw for our customers. However, we didn't have the test kitchens that the company has now, and finding the right blend was done by trial and error. A lot of people complained, especially in the early years, that the coffee wasn't strong enough. But when we moved into western Canada in the late 1970s, the opposite proved to be true: people there found the coffee too strong. In fact, in western Canada we cut back the 2.5-ounce package to 2.25 ounces in the hope of making it slightly weaker. But eventually we decided it was better to have one standard across the chain. Nonetheless, it took years for our coffee sales in western Canada to rival those of the rest of the country.

The coffee we serve today is essentially the same as it was when I took over the first store. You can't really tell the difference, despite all the testing the company has done of the coffee. The volume of coffee sold is incredible—more than 80 million pounds a year.

These days, the insatiable demand for Tim Hortons coffee makes certain it is always fresh. One of the issues I encountered when I took over the first restaurant was that the coffee would be left sitting around to go stale. I hated stale coffee and insisted it should always be fresh. Our initial goal was to ensure that a pot didn't sit for more than twenty minutes after it was brewed. Today, given the volume of customers going through the stores, a pot of coffee never even lasts for twenty minutes! That means it is always fresh. It was just part of our overriding philosophy. What is best? Hot pizza is always better than cold pizza. Fresh ice cream is always better than ice cream from a box. The same is true with coffee.

At some point, our brand became synonymous with great coffee. Once the chain became well established, you could have taken our coffee and served it at other restaurants, and people would have insisted it wasn't as good as the coffee served at Hortons. It is now a benchmark of quality and a barometer for all coffee in Canada. Coffee is the backbone of the company and, hopefully, it is one product that will not be tampered with by the present management team.

So many people in the food industry sell substandard product. In some cases, quality isn't the main concern. People who are willing to buy their meals at a convenience store, for example, aren't as concerned about the freshness of their food. That wasn't the customer we wanted to attract. We wanted to satisfy all of our customers who were looking for fresh food and were willing to pay a little bit more for a much higher quality product. The success and expansion of Tim Hortons would, over time, prove the theory was correct.

10

A MEMORIAL FOR TIM

One of the questions frequently asked of me is, How did the Tim Horton Foundation start, and when?

The Saturday prior to Tim's funeral—held on a Monday—I was with Ken Gariepy, a long-time friend of Tim and Lori's and the company's legal counsel. We were discussing the loss of our friend. About a year before his death, the three of us had purchased fifty acres of land in Hockley Valley near Orangeville, with the idea of perhaps developing it for recreational purposes. I said to Ken that it would be great to do something in Tim's memory, and he indicated that we could build a camp for underprivileged children on the property that we owned and that he was prepared to donate his one-third share in the land in Tim's estate if I did the same.

Ken said he was serious about the plan and suggested that we speak to Lori about her interest in the project. Lori thought it was a great idea, and with that in mind the three of us embraced the concept.

Though the plans were far from final, Reverend Gordon Griggs, an associate of the Hortons and their marriage counsellor for many years, announced at the funeral that a camp for financially disadvantaged youth would be set up in Tim's name. It may have been premature, but Reverend Griggs's public remarks gave some credibility to the fact the camp concept would go forward.

It didn't take long for some of the basics of the Memorial Camp to be developed. In our first organizational meeting, we decided to make an application for a registered foundation so that charitable tax receipts could be given to supporters. I don't recall now who designed the logo, but it was donated by the designer and represents Tim's two arms protecting a child.

Our desire was to cover all the costs associated with each child's stay, including transportation. If necessary, we were even prepared to pay to fly children from outside of Ontario. The notion of inclusiveness became a big part of the camp's philosophy and is a factor in the six camps that operate today.

In the weeks following the decision to construct a camp, we also made several visits to the proposed site with potential volunteers to determine the layout and decide what needed to be built to accommodate the expected children. In many ways, the site in Orangeville met all of our needs. It was close to Toronto, making it easy to get campers to and from the site, and Orangeville also had a hospital in case of emergencies.

A few months after the funeral, Ken called to talk about his concerns about moving forward with the camp.

"Ron, I became a little emotional after Tim's death, and I'm afraid I might have become a little carried away with the offer to give up my share of the property in Orangeville at Hockley Valley," he said. "I can't really afford to give up my interest."

I was shocked that he reneged on the concept because it was at his suggestion that we went forward with the idea. Ken's withdrawal from the project forced us to consider whether we could still go ahead with the camp. Lori and I met and decided that we would move forward with an alternate site. We then met with Ken to discuss a potential exchange of assets he had with us.

"Ken, you are a partner in the warehouse in Oakville. Why don't we trade you our shares in the Hockley Valley property for your shares in the warehouse, and that way Lori and I can go ahead with the camp without your involvement."

He agreed, but without the property in Hockley Valley, we didn't have a site for the camp. To address that issue, we sought out real-estate agents who specialized in the cottage country north of Toronto. The site for the camp needed to meet some specific requirements, which eliminated a lot of potential locations. The property needed to be easily accessible, have access to a lake, and be near a community with a hospital. After viewing many sites, we selected an old fishing camp on Lorimer Lake, near Parry Sound, as the home of the Tim Horton Memorial Camp. The buildings were derelict and would need a lot of work, but the place had most of the ingredients we were looking for. The purchase price was $75,000 with a low down payment and attractive terms for several years. We closed the deal in April and undertook the minimal requirements to open that summer. The Tim Horton Children's Foundation was born.

There was only one condition placed on the camp and foundation by Jim Blaney, Lori's legal adviser at the time. "Mrs. Horton cannot have any personal liability for anything that might occur at the camp, including financial liability of any kind," he said. It was therefore decided that Tim Donut Ltd. would essentially finance and maintain the camp.

As soon as the weather cleared in the spring of 1975, we gathered volunteers, friends, suppliers, company staff and store owners and began to renovate the facility. Though our labour force for projects at the camp in those early years was made up exclusively of volunteers, there were still costs associated with renovating the buildings. In exchange for the volunteered time, we supplied all of the food and beverages. Some of the volunteers may have thought they were coming just to have a good time, but that wasn't the case. If you worked at the camp, you were up at 6 a.m. and you continued until dark. All of the projects were well coordinated because there was so much to do.

"Damn, Ron, I never intended to come here to work twelve-hour days," one individual said during a tough day of construction.

"Well, then, you shouldn't have come," I replied.

But that doesn't mean we *didn't* have a good time. In the evenings we made sure there were activities to allow everyone to have some fun and unwind after their full day of work. It might have made more sense to contract out some of the work, but building, volunteering and working on the children's camps helped develop a team atmosphere among Tim Hortons' store owners, suppliers, staff and friends that surely benefited the company in the long run. I especially want to thank the late Carl Stewart and his family. He was the glue that held the camp together for over twenty years. I'll always be grateful for the outstanding contributions that made the first camp a reality—led by my good friends Layton Coulter, George and Dorothy McGlinchey, A. J. Thompson, George Rumble, Jim Flemming, Ed and Florence Mattatall, Eldon and Doreen Fawcett, and so many others that escape my memory. Each of them gave so very unselfishly at the start-up, which turned out to be a very significant undertaking, but it couldn't have possibly developed into what it is today without the pioneers on the first camp. It was the training ground for what has become such a hugely successful way to help young people to enjoy themselves and see our country in a special way. I believe that many of them learn more about each other and themselves, and in turn, raise their own self-esteem.

In the process of selecting our campers, we devised a plan to make the store owners responsible for finding underprivileged children for each of the weeks the camp operated during the summer. By sharing the workload, it made it easier to find children that met the criteria from broad geographic regions; we also approached groups such as the police, schools, teachers and organizations such as Big Brothers and Big Sisters and the Children's Aid Society for help in the search. To transport the children to the camp from the Toronto area, we purchased an old school bus, and Tim's brother Jerry arranged to have it painted blue and white and include the camp's distinctive logo. Even though we were amateurs when it came to running the camp, in our first summer we hosted thirty-two children at each of the five camp sessions—160 in all. Given our inexperience, the inaugural year went surprisingly well.

It was important that there was no publicity or fanfare attached to this endeavour, because my feeling was that children did not need to be reminded of their status in life. Everything was handled with discretion. We hired a school principal as director, with teachers and people we knew as camp counsellors.

We muddled through in those early years, but by 1979 we concluded that the camp would benefit from having a professional involved. With that in mind, we hired Peter Moffatt and his wife, Cheryl. Peter had a great deal of experience working with camps in the U.S. With Peter taking a leadership role and further refining what the Memorial

Camp was about, we were able to move ahead with further improvements to the facilities.

Among the issues we had to immediately address was the old school bus. It had proven to be wholly unreliable and had had several breakdowns. The foundation's nominal budgets could not afford to purchase and maintain a new bus, so the TDL group bought a new MCI bus with air conditioning and had it painted in the same dark brown colours used on the trucks that hauled goods for TDL across the country. After the summer season, when camp let out, we would use the bus for philanthropic projects such as transporting seniors or children to different events and for public relations. The new bus and its community involvement helped draw attention to the relationship between TDL, Tim Hortons store owners and the Memorial Camp. The tradition has continued. Today there are five buses.

In the years after we established the Memorial Camp, we completed many building projects and renovations, including a caretaker's quarters, new bunkhouses, recreation centre, marina and director's and camp counsellors' cabins. The tenth anniversary of the camp was celebrated with an official dedication to Tim, and was attended by many of his friends and people who supported the camp, including store owners and former teammates of Tim's, like Dick Duff, Dave Keon, Carl Brewer, Frank Mahovlich and George Armstrong. Wally Crouter from CFRB radio acted as master of ceremonies. Dick Trainor, by this time a judge who also was a director of the Tim Horton Children's Foundation, gave a marvellous speech about his long friendship with Tim. Mike Harris, who would later become a great premier of Ontario, was also there. He was a great supporter of the foundation and is now a director. Mr. Justice Roy McMurtry also made a great speech about Tim and the work of the foundation.

My appreciation and interest in the camp grew as I gained a better sense of what it might accomplish and the impact it was having on the children who attended. Many of the campers came from difficult circumstances and were thrilled to be able to get away from them for a few days and enjoy the natural surroundings. It didn't take long for all of us to see the difference the camp was making in their lives.

It was very expensive to build and renovate the camp, so our fund-raising efforts became critical to the camp's success right from the start. The primary sources of donations were store owners, suppliers, friends and Tim Donut Ltd. and staff. We also placed coin boxes in each location, which allowed customers to contribute loose change in support of the foundation. The only hitch was that all of these donations made in quarters, dimes and nickels had to be counted. For years, my executive assistant, Michele Allison, other staff and I would count and roll all of the buckets of change that came in from stores across Canada. It was time-consuming, but knowing where the money was going made it all worthwhile. Today, it's a relief to have the sophisticated coin-counting equipment that is now available, given the millions of dollars raised through the boxes annually.

We called in favours from our suppliers to get them to donate various products used at camp during the summer. As well, we approached our store owners and asked if they would contribute one-half of one percent of our advertising budget to the camp each year. I then matched the amount, which helped give the camp a strong financial backing. In order to garner as much support for the camp and the foundation as we could, we also held golf tournaments each summer and Old-Timers' hockey games in the winter.

In those early days, it was made clear to our restaurant owners and employees that Tim Hortons wasn't to be seen to be gaining anything from its support of the foundation. It was intended as pure philan-thropy, and no one involved was to expect any kind of reward for their participation.

It didn't take long for the foundation to grow well beyond our expec-tations. The impact we were having on the children who attended our camps was amazing, and it prompted Gary O'Neill to inquire about starting a camp in Atlantic Canada. We hadn't originally intended to expand the camp concept beyond the Memorial Camp in Parry Sound, but we considered Gary's request. Unfortunately, I didn't consult with Lori about it. This was probably a source of annoyance for her and may have contributed to the personal problems we later experienced.

Gary refused to take no for an answer. "We should have our own camp in the Maritimes, Ron," he told me. "We are always taking kids from out here to the Ontario camp. We should have kids out here as well."

"But bringing kids from the Maritimes was exactly what the camp was intended to do," I told him.

"Well, the owners out here would like to have their own camp."

After gauging a sense of the support we'd receive from the owners, we determined we would proceed. We looked at many properties in New Brunswick, Prince Edward Island and Nova Scotia. After all of this scouting, we felt we had nailed down a great location in Nova Scotia, but the deal fell through. Instead, in 1986 we ended up pur-chasing a rural property from Georg Vogel on Malagash Bay, near my hometown of Tatamagouche, which was also where Gary was from. Vogel had come to Canada from Germany and intended to farm the property. Instead, after some insistence from his significant other, Maureen Holmes, he sold the property to us for $225,000, though he stayed actively involved in the project after the sale, helping to manage construction of the camp. The land we purchased had a farmhouse, a large barn and two other buildings on 245 acres of land. However, a lot of work lay ahead of us before we could hope to bring children to Nova Scotia. It didn't take long to convert the barn on the property into a building to house many of the volunteers. One of the other buildings was made into a cookhouse to prepare and serve meals on site during construction. Several people played key roles in the development of the second camp. My cousin, Dale Jollymore, who had built many of the Tim Hortons stores in Nova Scotia and New Brunswick, took responsibility for the construction of all of the buildings, and Maureen Holmes was a tremendous asset by contributing and arranging the food for the many volunteers.

By this time, both the company and the foundation were more secure financially than they had been when the concept was launched in 1974. We had more than 300 Tim Hortons stores, versus the forty we had when we created the first camp, a factor that made raising money much easier. The funding of the site work was done with bank financing. This camp was much costlier than the first; construction cost more than $5 million, including all of the equipment and furnishings as well as the waterfront marina with sailboats, rescue boat, pontoon boat and canoes. The camp opened in 1988, and we received significant support from the Atlantic store owners, who donated the gross sales from their stores over a twenty-four-hour period to the construction of the main dining hall, which cost more than $1 million. It was something they would do for the next few years, even though it was tough financially for some of the lower-volume stores. In many ways, the Atlantic Canada store owners were the founders of the national Camp Day Canada fundraiser that still exists today. And today, the store owners throughout the system continue, through many endeavours, to give so unselfishly of their time and revenues to the foundation.

This was truly an evolutionary time for the camp concept and the Tim Horton Children's Foundation. As our financial situation improved, it was determined that the foundation should also have a more stable governance structure. We decided the foundation should have an outside board of directors, and the initial group included Douglas Christie, Roy Moore, Bill Hunter, George and Dorothy McGlinchey and Dick Trainor. As the foundation grew, the outside directors included some well-known business people and store owners, like the Honourable Michael Harris, Keith Conklin, Jean Pigott, Brian Williams, Gary O'Neill, John Hoey, David Sobey, William Fitz, Dale Jollymore, Don Schroeder, Ian Murray, Wayne Newson, Miles Mattatall, Scott Cahill and Andrew McCaughey. We also began developing a vision for what the children's foundation should become. The idea was to expand the concept to include four camps in total, one for each of Canada's geographic regions.

The third camp was planned for western Canada, near the Rockies. John Barber, who was managing the real-estate division in the west at the time, met with Ed Marshall, the director general of Kananaskis Provincial Park, north of Calgary. Marshall, a notable Calgary businessman, had been in charge of the park from 1978 until his departure from the position. We would need to convince him of the value of our plan to put a camp in the park, which had been created by the Alberta government in 1977 to give the province's residents a mountain recreation area that was significantly different from the commercialized national parks of Banff and Jasper. Our hope was the third children's camp could be created in such a way that it would fit within the park's mandate.

Marshall decided it would be best if he sent two of his senior staff, forest protection officer Kelly O'Shea and Kananaskis country director Fred Wilmot, to Nova Scotia and Ontario to see exactly how the existing camps functioned. Once in Tatamagouche, the park staff experienced all the camp had to offer, including an opportunity to meet with Premier John Buchanan and enjoy a sail aboard the *Bluenose II*, which happened to be in Pictou Harbour at the time. After leaving Nova Scotia, we went to the camp in Parry Sound so that Ed's people could take a tour. The visit was a success, and they approved the concept and put together a committee to evaluate properties. Marshall, Henry Svazas and I spent a day in a helicopter flying over all the locations they had identified. We picked a 150-acre site situated beneath the wondrous mountains.

Ed was a great host and had a love of the province that he shared with us. When we saw the property in Kananaskis country with Bob Jenkins, manager of planning and design, it was the hands-down winner. The challenge now became to get permits to build the camp. Ed was marvellous in leading us through the process and also proved very helpful in expediting permits for the land and the buildings from the Kananaskis board so that we could begin construction immediately. There were very strict rules covering design and construction materials, which we conformed to on all counts. Construction started in 1989, and the next year we held an event called the East-West Challenge, which involved volunteer teams from eastern and western Canada. Each team had to build two bunkhouses and compete to see who could construct theirs the fastest. The western team put up a quarter of prime Alberta beef against 250 pounds of Nova Scotia lobsters from the eastern team. It rained constantly that week, and the construction site was a mud bath. In spite of this, the volunteers worked hard and constructed all four of the bunkhouses. The competition was declared a tie, and we all came together to enjoy the beef and lobsters.

The third Tim Horton Children's Camp, this one built in a ranch style, was established in July 1991; we celebrated the grand opening with the company's restaurant owners during our national convention, held in Calgary that year.

The last of the four camps we planned to open was built in Quyon, Quebec, not far from Ottawa. We approached the federal government and Jean Pigott, chair of the National Capital Commission, about opening a camp to be ready for 1994. We told Jean about the success we'd had with our first three camps and our plans of sharing the capital city with children from across the country. She gave us her enthusiastic endorsement and helped us find a site that would be suitable for our purposes in creating what would be called Camp des Voyageurs. I first met Jean Pigott at her office when I was in Ottawa and she was chair of the National Capital Commission. When she heard of our idea for the Children's Camp, she was very excited and thought a camp somewhere on the National Capital Commission property would be ideal. She offered several locations, and the one that we finally accepted was on Pontiac Bay in Quyon.

The first day there, we flew in on an amphibian aircraft, landed on shallow water and waded ashore. It was a wonderful site that once belonged to a camp owned by the Presbyterian church. When they no longer needed it, they donated it to the NCC. We were prepared to pay $50,000 for the property, but were told the asking price was $100,000. We offered to acquire the land on the condition that, if we no longer used it as a camp for underprivileged children, the site would revert back to the National Capital Commission. Jean helped us present our offer to the NCC, and we soon acquired the property.

As with the other camps, there was a tremendous amount of volunteer work and support in the planning and construction of the facilities. People came from across the country to support us in creating all aspects of the camp. One interesting thing that happened was that we ran afoul of Quebec labour laws. At that time, construction projects had to be completed by construction workers from Quebec. Because we had many volunteers coming in from other provinces, the camp was temporarily closed for not abiding by the regulations—even though our workers were volunteers.

Like the previous three camps, the Quyon facility had a distinct motif. In keeping with its setting, it was designed in a French-Canadian style, with a nod to the culture and diversity of the province. The camp opened in 1994, which coincided with our national convention in Ottawa, and Governor General Ray Hnatyshyn was among the dignitaries in attendance. Precision military parachutists landed on the site, the Governor General's military band performed, there was a flyby of the Snowbirds, and the RCMP Musical Ride made an appearance. Since Jean Pigott had been so helpful and dedicated to establishing the facility, we had purchased the land on one condition: that she join the board of directors of the Tim Horton Children's Foundation. She agreed.

That was supposed to be our final children's camp, but by this time TDL was involved with Wendy's. Wendy's founder Dave Thomas had taken notice of the success of our camps and suggested that we bring American children north to experience Canada. The idea was such a hit with the children that we set to work on opening a fifth camp, to be located in the United States. Thomas was friends with Wallace Wilkinson, who had been the governor of Kentucky and who was instrumental in bringing the camp to his state. We agreed to lease property on Green River Lake, near Campbellsville, south of Louisville. The camp, which was the first one built entirely by outside contractors, was opened in 2001, just as I was ending my tenure with TDL (I remained senior chairman of the foundation after leaving the TDL board).

Nor did we stop there. Earlier in my career, I'd been introduced to Gil and Molly Henderson through mutual friends Alec and Ruth Murray. I became fast friends with the Hendersons, who owned Onondaga Farms in St. George, Ontario, a town near Brantford. They regularly welcomed me into their beautiful home, and they were always gracious hosts. Over the years, Gil and I enjoyed many hunting and fishing trips together.

In 1998, Molly became sick and I received a call in Florida from Gil.

"Molly is in the hospital and she's not coming out," he said. "I'm not going to let her make the journey alone."

I was shocked when I got the news, and told him I was heading back up to Canada the next day, so I would see them as soon as I arrived. I went to the hospital in Brantford and found that Molly had little lung capacity and needed 80 percent oxygen. Despite that, she was alert. She told me that since they did not have children, they were worried about what might happen to their lovely home and farm in the country. We had spoken a few times about possibly making it a Tim Horton Children's Camp so that many children could enjoy what the Hendersons had built over the years. They were very much respected in their community, in particular for their interest in and involvement with the environment, for which they had won many awards.

We agreed in principle that we would convert the farm into a camp, a commitment I reinforced to Molly before she passed away in February 1999. At that time, because we had already committed to the camp in Kentucky, there were no immediate plans to build at Onondaga. I was very eager that the Onondaga camp be built, but the directors of the Tim Horton Children's Foundation—Drew McCaughey and a couple of others—were reluctant to move ahead; we were still dealing with the costs of the other recent sites and money was tight. We decided to hold a board meeting at Gil's place so that all of the outside directors and store owners could see the property. Gil and I had an opportunity to make our pitch and present our thoughts on having our next camp at Onondaga. Because of my position on the board, we decided that it would be a conflict of interest for me to vote on the project and that the directors should meet in camera. I agreed to abide by whatever decision they arrived at. Gil and I left the meeting for almost an hour, which indicates there was a great deal of discussion among the directors.

Though I am not sure exactly what happened behind the scenes, I believe that a few of the store owners, including Scott Cahill, spoke very passionately to the outside directors in support of turning Onondaga into a camp. They must have been very persuasive, because the board approved the request and decided to go ahead. Gil and I were called back into the meeting and we were told of the decision to proceed. The property was worth approximately $4 million, with one of the most significant costs being the Henderson home. I mentioned that I was prepared to purchase the home personally and in turn donate it to the foundation on the condition that Gil would continue to live and remain in the home for as long as he wanted. Even with all of the considerable costs associated with building the camp, I feel the result—with funds raised from the store owners and myself—was a marvellous facility.

At first, we thought we'd postpone the construction for a couple of years until we could raise more money and reduce some of the debt associated with the Campbellsville camp. But I prevailed upon the board to set a goal of opening it in 2002. We immediately commissioned architectural drawings and began to make plans. As with all of the camps, a tremendous amount of work went into the project, and it really is one of the jewels of the Tim Horton Children's Foundation.

Of the six, the Onondaga camp was the most expensive to build, largely because it has many amenities that are not found in the others and because it was intended to serve as the base of operations for the foundation. For instance, this is the place where camp staff go to receive leadership training from the foundation. Because of its proximity to some of the major cities of southern Ontario—Toronto, Hamilton, Kitchener—many outside groups, such as boards of education, also make use of the facilities and training programs. The camp also operates year-round. As a result, it remains the most used facility.

In 2002, at the grand opening, we dedicated the main lodge to Molly and unveiled two paintings of Molly and Gil. The creation of Onondaga was a tremendous accomplishment for Don Schroeder, the president of the foundation, as well as all of the people who put their efforts into the project. They should be applauded for having the strength and vision to open two camps so quickly.

Though they started out as a simple dream to recognize our company's namesake, the camps have flourished and grown profoundly. And, to our great surprise, they have been very well received, and supported, by the public at large. Every year, Canadians open their wallets and purses on Camp Day, the company's fundraiser whereby the proceeds from every cup of coffee sold in Tim Hortons stores is donated to the Tim Horton Children's Foundation. In a twenty-four-hour period, the fundraiser generates stunning amounts of money—$6.4 million in 2005, and $7.2 million in 2006.

This money has allowed many children to attend the camps and, through their voices and experiences, share with their families and friends the profound effect the camps have had on their young lives. The Tim Hortons camps have become synonymous with the chain, and the company has been very fortunate to receive letters from many individuals who attended the camps, learned leadership skills, and went on to lead outstanding lives and give back to their own communities.

One of the remarkable things about the camps is that they continue to support the ideals and mission that we developed and fostered in the very beginning. And when Wendy's took over TDL in 1996, the agreement stipulated that it would honour the commitment to support the foundation as if I were still in charge.

There have been so many things I've been pleased to have had a hand in developing or creating during my time at TDL and Tim Hortons, but it may turn out that the children's camps are my legacy. They remain one of the achievements I'm most proud of—they're an integral part of the fabric of Tim Hortons, and just another demonstration of the company's commitment to this country and its communities. More than 10,000 children attend the camps every year, and although we do not know the exact number of children we have hosted over the last thirty-two years, the number would be several hundred thousand. It's a remarkable accomplishment for a concept with such humble beginnings.

11

FLYING HIGH

By the time TDL opened its 100th store in Thunder Bay in 1978, I had begun to worry that the company had grown too large to be managed by a single person and to wonder whether I had the skills to take the company to the next level. When a company reaches a certain size, professional management needs to come on board to help see it to the next level. The idea of one day operating so many stores had never crossed my mind during the early years of Tim Hortons, but we were now well on our way towards becoming a national chain. I was going to need support if that dream was to become a reality.

To that end, I hired George Haggerty, who had been a vice-president at Dunkin' Donuts, to work for TDL. I'd met George during our negotiations to sell TDL in 1975, and we had maintained our friendship over the years. The aim was to have George, who had been involved in operations at Dunkin' Donuts, standardize TDL's management procedures.

It soon became apparent that there was a problem: George's management style was not similar to that which had preceded him. He was insistent that we begin documenting everything the company did, which led to a lot of paperwork. TDL's operation had never been run that formally. Also, George would put in long days at the office, occasionally arriving as early as 6 a.m. and not leaving until late in the evening—something else that differed dramatically from the status quo at TDL. Senior staff at TDL also began to log more hours, and to work through weekends. Not surprisingly, we started to get some resistance from some of our top people, and it became apparent that the company risked losing some of our best management people if the long hours continued. Within a year of George's arrival, perhaps due to the staff's unhappiness, problems started arising in the business. Some senior staff I trusted began to complain about his management style. I was concerned about the ramifications of these issues, and determined that the best thing for TDL would be for TDL and George to part company, and I stepped back in to manage the company. In the interest of preserving TDL's corporate culture, from George's departure onwards, the company always looked to promote internally, rather than hire external candidates. Improvements were made during Haggerty's tenure, but TDL was still not a particularly well-managed company after he left.

Though the company was making progress in its march towards becoming a national chain, Tim Hortons continued to struggle in several parts of the country—for instance, in western Canada. In retrospect, many of the problems that faced our stores there can be attributed to the differences in the ways people consume food at restaurants in North America. It is almost as if you could draw a north-south dividing line, from the western boundary of Ontario, straight down through the United States; certain types of restaurants work well east of that boundary, but fail to connect with customers west of it. Dunkin' Donuts, for example, had a very difficult time building a business in the western United States; meanwhile, in Canada, the Swiss Chalet and St. Hubert rotisserie chicken chains found it hard to make inroads into the western provinces.

So it was for Tim Hortons. But despite the initial setbacks, TDL stuck with these stores. In many respects, a lot of the credit for the company's eventual success in the west belongs to the early store owners, who persevered even when the situation looked bleak and it was a struggle to find regular customers. TDL's philosophy also helped: other operations would most surely have forced the franchisees out when bills went unpaid. They would undoubtedly have resold the franchises, creating the same cycle of failure that the first owners faced. Instead, as we had done before, we forgave royalties, enabling stores to remain open through the fallow periods.

The disappointing performance of the restaurants in western Canada made it clear that what had worked in Ontario and Atlantic Canada was not completely transferable to the rest of the country. I came to the conclusion that we had to be less centralized, and that splitting the business up into geographic regions would be best. The aim was to open regional offices that would be hands-on, responding to the specific concerns of store owners. At the time, Jim Rushak was a store owner in Milton, Ontario, and he had done a tremendous job of taking a difficult store and turning it into a great operation, dramatically increasing sales. I approached Jim and told him how impressed I was with his work. By the early 1980s, he became vice-president of the company's western operations, overseeing all matters in real estate, franchise sales, legal, marketing and distribution.

"Jim, the system just doesn't seem to work in western Canada," I told him. "We are seeing mounting losses, but I'm prepared to continue investing over the next five years to keep the stores open. If it isn't working by then, we'll have to consider our options." In reality, failure wasn't an option. TDL would not be able to make Tim Hortons into a national brand if it couldn't crack the western market.

Unlike Quebec, where we faced stiff competition, the problem in western Canada was that customers weren't embracing Tim Hortons' products, including our coffee. However, we continued to support the owners of the struggling stores, even as they lost money, in the hope that a strong operation would emerge. In time, the strategy proved to be correct. Meanwhile, Jim did a superb job of building a great team, and in short order he'd not only turned things around, he had the chain's western region growing at the same rate as our eastern stores. Jim was an adept communicator, particularly when it came to articulating the philosophy of the chain. He worked very closely with all the store owners, and was also gifted at sorting out the strong franchisees from those who were having difficulty meeting TDL's expectations. In those instances where he could not get a store owner to change, they were asked to leave the company.

Similarly, our ambitions to break into the American market started slowly. Though the company's recent move into the U.S. has been well documented, most people don't realize that Tim Hortons opened its first U.S. location twenty-five years ago. The first store south of the border opened in Florida in 1981. The rationale was that we would attract Canadian snowbirds who travelled south every winter; they were expected to create a strong enough customer base while local residents became familiar with the brand. The store opened on Atlantic Boulevard in Pompano Beach and did manage to catch the interest of

Americans as well as Canadians escaping the cold winter in the north. A second store opened on Federal Highway in Deerfield, and it suffered in the hot summer months, though sales increased in the cooler months. These stores lasted for fourteen years before they were finally closed. They still operate as donut shops today, though not under the Tim Hortons banner.

However, the company did make an impression in Florida. During the late 1980s, I was making a business trip to the area. At the time, a place had opened up in Fort Lauderdale that billed itself as a "topless donut store." In other words, topless waitresses served the customers. I decided to check out the store, which was on the way to the airport. Sure enough, there was a waitress walking around absolutely topless. I ordered a cup of coffee and a donut. Each was a dollar, significantly more than they would typically sell for. The donut turned out to be quite good.

"Do you make the donuts here?" I asked the waitress.

"No," she replied. "We buy them at the Tim Hortons store not far from here."

Our next foray into the U.S. was a venture that was recommended by a friend of mine, Don Schroeder. He felt that Hilton Head and Beaufort, South Carolina, had similarities to the markets served by our Canadian stores, but the stores we opened there failed to find even the limited success of the Florida store. To Don's credit, he took full responsibility for the planning and financing of the stores. Unfortunately, they didn't become profitable; it was difficult to attract either employees or customers, leading to large financial losses and forcing us to close the stores. In hindsight, the lessons learned were worth the experiment: we found that warm, semi-tropical areas are not well suited to a business selling coffee and donuts.

Of course, in the current climate, the U.S. provides a great opportunity for Tim Hortons. Though few are aware of it, many of the company's border stores have been quite successful. Using the same strategy that we devised when we opened stores around Hamilton, we quietly branched out to Western New York in 1992. The region's proximity to Ontario meant that many of the residents were already familiar with Tim Hortons and its products. That in turn meant that the company did not have to spend an inordinate amount to promote the brand. Ken Broderick, a former NHL goaltender who now works for Tim Hortons, and two partners were behind the Buffalo move.

Our move into the U.S. occurred just as the donut industry in Ontario was becoming saturated by competitors offering inferior products and involved in elaborate schemes to sell franchises. I grew very concerned about the industry that we were in. Though the concept of donut stores was new to Ontario when Tim Hortons first opened, by the early 1980s, it had become the haunt of pretenders who were more interested in selling substandard franchises and products than in quality.

One of the best examples was Robin's Donuts, a company formed by employees who left Tim Hortons in 1975. The business was created by George Spicer, who had been my right-hand man at Tim Hortons for several years after leaving our flour supplier to join us. During his time with us, he hired a man named Harvey Caldwell. Caldwell was bright, and he used his time at TDL to learn as much about the company as he could. Though I never suspected that anything was awry, only a year after Caldwell arrived, he and Spicer quit at the same time and announced they were opening a new donut store, appropriately called Robin's Donuts, in Thunder Bay. When the store opened, it looked uncannily like a Tim Hortons, which wasn't surprising when you consider that Caldwell had used our plans and suppliers in launching the new enterprise. Everything was copied, and the business even proceeded to poach some of Tim Hortons' employees. Though we gave some consideration to launching a lawsuit against the new competitor, I felt the company's decision to locate in Thunder Bay would marginalize it.

While I didn't like what Caldwell had done, I remained friendly with Spicer. Soon after the store in Thunder Bay opened, I approached George and asked what the game plan was for Robin's Donuts.

"Look, Ron, we only intend to open the one store," he told me. That policy didn't last long, of course, and in time they managed to open more than 200 stores. Tim Hortons' 100th store opened in Thunder Bay with the intent of competing against their operation. Despite the presence of Robin's, our new store, which was the first Tim Hortons in the city, did very well.

Though Caldwell took the look and many of the ideas behind Tim Hortons with him when he founded Robin's Donuts, he couldn't find a way to deliver the quality or consistency that had become our trademarks. Like many competitors that followed, it appeared his main goal was to sell franchises rather than build a great and lasting business. Robin's would grow to become one of our larger Canadian competitors, but its stores did low volumes, and in time it ended up in bankruptcy.

Robin's Donuts was just one example of the competitors who attempted to rival Tim Hortons as we expanded across the country. In other cases, chains would spring up and people would buy into the concept, thinking that they were purchasing franchises that sold donuts and would become healthy businesses, when in fact they were investing in sketchy organizations that would regularly go bankrupt.

What Robin's and these fly-by-night operations had in common was that they failed to recognize that a strong chain is built one link at a time. If you don't try to sell a solid, proven business to your franchisees, and instead focus solely on selling franchises, you're doomed to failure.

One thing that the rise of Robin's Donuts did accomplish was to convince me it was time to distance Tim Hortons from the overheated donut market. It seemed as if every time Tim Hortons launched a new advertising campaign or opened a new store, all the other donut operations in the area would also benefit. These competitors were shameless about aping Tim Hortons' products and would copy everything from Timbits to the "Roll Up the Rim" campaign in later years. I came to the conclusion that donuts would no longer be at the core of our business. From the business's start, the parent company had been called Tim Donut Ltd., while the store signage read "Tim Hortons Donuts."* From this point on, the stores were simply to be known as "Tim Hortons."

Having made that decision, the question became how best to alter the business's branding so as to reflect this new strategy. Our logo, with its two ovals, was well recognized throughout Canada by this time, and we planned to continue to use it even as we rebranded the company. There was much discussion over a catchphrase that would be representative of the business while also being short enough to fit on our signs. Finally, I decided upon a distillation of what had been the company's philosophy from the start: "Always Fresh." Even the parent company would get a makeover, as Tim Donut Ltd. had its name abbreviated to TDL.

---

* There were several variations on the Tim Hortons name used in the early years of the company. For example, Jim Charade used Tim Horton's Do-Nuts in some of the Toronto stores, before the business became standardized under the Tim Horton's Donuts brand. The apostrophe was dropped in order to bring consistency to the company's packaging when it entered the Quebec market.

In our mind, "Always Fresh" wasn't just a comment on Tim Hortons' products. It reflected the entire company's attitude. The restaurants would be clean and well run. The parking lots would be tidy. We would change and alter our menu on a regular basis. The entire business would be "always fresh."

In recent years, when I speak to business schools about Tim Hortons, students often ask me what attributes were most responsible for the chain's success. Many people feel there must be some secret strategy that set Tim Hortons apart from its competition. But the "Always Fresh" slogan, and all that it represents, went a long way to help build the company's reputation.

People often incorrectly assume that it was a big step for us to remove the word "donuts" from the company's name. Clearly it was, in terms of branding, but the move was calculated to more clearly represent where the business was heading. Though donuts might have been the company's drawing card in 1964, by 1985 Tim Hortons was really successful because of how well its operations were run. Donuts were no longer the most significant part of our menu. Coffee, and a myriad of other products, had surpassed them. By downplaying the donuts, we were able to promote our brand, as opposed to one product. As I had suggested to Tim in 1966, the name Tim Hortons had to be the company's principal focus.

Besides using my "Always Fresh" branding, there would be other slogans, the majority of which would be the product of the advertising agencies we employed. Not all of them were winners. For a while, for instance, we used, "They're always fresh because you keep eating them." It was one I personally didn't care for, and in time it disappeared. Others, like "Your friend along the way" and "You've always got time for Tim Hortons," really struck a chord with the public. In

1987, soon after the "You've always got time" slogan was introduced, I travelled to Fort McMurray, Alberta, to scout a possible location for a new store. Once the company jet, which had the tail number "Donut 1," landed, the pilot was concerned about the temperature, which was hovering around -40 degrees Celsius.

"Don't be long, Boss, or we might have problems," he said. "There's nowhere to park the plane indoors."

We did a quick drive around and I returned to the airport. As I often did, I asked the pilot to call the control tower and ask if we could have time to circle Fort McMurray for a few minutes to look at real estate before we headed back to Calgary.

The reply was unexpected: "We always have time for Tim Hortons," the air traffic controller said.

After the sale to Wendy's in 1996, there was a renewed push to expand Tim Hortons into the U.S. One of the challenges the company faced was that many potential customers were unaware of the chain's ubiquity north of the border, and therefore would not know what products were sold in Tim Hortons restaurants. One of the potential solutions that some within Wendy's offered up was a return to defining the company by a specific product, like donuts. But brands tied to a specific product are limited, and eventually Wendy's was convinced not to change Tim Hortons' branding.

ooooo

The struggles with the western Canadian stores hit the company at a time when it could simply not afford to have its restaurants underperform. In 1980, TDL was hit by an economic storm. The chain was in the midst of its westward expansion when inflation started to rise dramatically. At about the same time, interest rates soared above 20 percent, which was particularly troublesome for TDL, since we were borrowing much of the capital we used for expansion.

Though the system remained strong in Ontario, Nova Scotia, New Brunswick and Prince Edward Island, the losses in the western provinces were becoming a significant issue for the company. Some of the stores were taking in less than half of their sales targets, and therefore lacked the cash flow to pay their rent. Others were having trouble paying for supplies. Their cash flow problems became the company's: every dollar the franchisees couldn't pay back on the costs of building their stores contributed to the debt that TDL had to service—and at much higher interest rates than we could afford.

The problems mounted, and by 1981, with interest rates still escalating, TDL was in danger of running out of capital. Our debt, which floated at the prime interest rate plus one percentage point, had soared to more than $10 million, and the company, for the first time in its history, was forced to lay off staff. Our construction division saw drastic cuts, and we could not afford to take out loans to acquire new property; instead, in order to keep the system growing, we reverted to leasing buildings and land.

The Mercantile Bank of Canada, which had backed my bid to buy Lori's stake in TDL and had bankrolled the company's expansion in the late 1970s, never realized how close TDL came to the brink of financial ruin in this period. That is because, although money was tight, the company never failed to meet its debt obligations. However, coming up with the money to pay the bank was often difficult, especially when it came to refinancing some of our high-end debt. We had to be creative in finding ways to repay some of our loans.

Though those were tough years, the fact that Tim Hortons survived demonstrates the strength of the system we had created. It was a chain that could prevail, even if weak links became apparent. Successful stores were able to more than compensate for the underperformers, allowing us to make it through difficult times. By 1983, inflation rates had subsided, ending TDL's cash crunch. The experience did teach me an important lesson: I vowed to never again put the business at risk by adding more debt than the company could handle comfortably. That would remain a policy for the next decade, and due to the business's outstanding cash flow, which was enhanced by the high demand for new franchises, TDL was able to carry very limited debt from that point forward.

ooooo

Being a goal-oriented company, once we had our debt issues in hand, the focus went right back to expanding the company. We took a major step in this direction in late 1985, when TDL purchased its first jet. The acquisition coincided with the opening of the 250th Tim Hortons store, in Oakville. Airplane travel had long been a fact of life at TDL. Initially, of course, our operations were centred in Hamilton and the vicinity. But by the time the company was only five years old, it had grown to include outlets in eastern Ontario, in Cornwall, Brockville, Kingston and Belleville. All that travel on Highway 401 was tiring and time-consuming. Owning a plane would allow me to save time visiting restaurants and scouting prospective sites for new stores. I also decided that it would help if I got my pilot's licence. It wasn't that flying was a fascination of mine; rather, it was a pragmatic move. Later, our expansion plans would take us even farther afield, into areas that weren't easily reached via commercial airlines; our executives would save a lot of time flying directly to these towns, time they might have to spend waiting in airport terminals for connecting flights.

It didn't take me long to get my licence, though I was not an instrument-rated pilot. By law, I was only allowed to fly under visual flight rules (VFR), meaning I had to be able to see the ground in order to fly the plane. Of course, given the amount I used the plane to travel, I occasionally ended up in circumstances that tested all of my abilities as a pilot, especially when I was still climbing the learning curve.

I recall one very scary incident when George Spicer and I were flying to Quebec City in our light Twin Piper Aztec. Although the forecast for the area allowed for VFR flight, we came into a very heavy snow storm near Quebec City and they closed the airport. They informed us that Trois-Rivierès was visual so I proceeded to do a 180-degree turn and managed to get us into not one but two spirals. Because I wasn't instrument rated, I made the absolute error of not keeping my eyes on the instruments. Needless to say we survived but it scared the hell out of us and it led me into a much needed course on instrument flying.

I remember having another issue flying in the early years of the company, though this one had nothing to do with weather. On this occasion, I was flying Tim and Dick Trainor, a close associate of the two of us, back from Sudbury. Both Tim and Dick had consumed a few drinks before and during the flight and after we took off, Tim decided he was going to fly the airplane just as we were overtop Ken Geriepy's cottage at Hockley Valley in Orangeville. He took the stick and made several wild movements. I quickly took control of the plane from him, but I don't think he realized the moments of terror we experienced with his manoeuvres.

Over time I became much more confident as a pilot. I logged thousands of miles and hundreds of hours piloting a plane on Tim Hortons business, and I never once had an accident. The planes were a valuable business resource, and I loved the freedom they provided. Flying solo gave me the free time to think about the business and consider my options. The planes were also used regularly to scout locations for new stores. It was not uncommon to fly over a small city or town, with several executives from TDL, getting a bird's-eye view that helped us decide where the best location might be to open a new store.

However, following Tim's death, I became acutely aware that I should probably not fly solo as often as I had been. I hired a pilot, Emil Meshberg, who brought a high level of professionalism and safety to our travel. He would fly the TDL planes for more than two decades, and he was the one who came up with the call signs on the planes' tails: "Donut 1" and, when a second plane was added, "Donut 2."

As TDL expanded, it became increasingly important to have planes that could fly faster and farther. With that in mind, the company purchased its first propjet in 1979, to shorten the travel time between Ontario and Atlantic Canada. By 1985, we felt the need for a full-fledged jet aircraft for the longer flights to western Canada. A jet would also be able to hold more people. I set my sights on a Cessna S550 Citation S/II. There was an element of prestige in owning a jet, and although it was an expensive purchase that was made with a degree of trepidation, Tim Hortons' growth convinced me it was a necessary tool that the company could afford.

It should have been one of the highlights of my life when we went down to Wichita, Kansas, to pick up the plane. After making the final payment on the Citation, the company took us up for a test flight. I flew the plane to 30,000 feet, doing some elaborate moves, including some hard turns and emergency descents.

But once back in Hamilton, I went into a depression. I had set certain goals in my life, many of which I had never felt I would achieve, but which gave me something to strive for. Having my own jet was one of those aims and, having accomplished that, I found myself disappointed. I had been operating Tim Hortons for twenty years, taking the company from a single-store operation to more than 250 restaurants. Tim Hortons had survived the death of its namesake and assaults from competitors and had emerged stronger and more vibrant than ever. Owning a jet symbolized the success of the vision that built TDL and Tim Hortons, but it raised a vital question for me: What was there left to do? It seems silly now to have had those feelings, but at the time I had fulfilled most of the goals I had set for my business life. It took several months to refocus my energy on new goals. One of those new objectives would be to open 1,000 Tim Hortons stores within a decade.

12

HORTONS, HOCKEY AND HAMILTON

Given the chain's namesake, it must seem to some that there is a direct link between professional hockey and Tim Hortons, but I never had any desire to be involved with the National Hockey League. And even though Tim Hortons had long been aligned as a sponsor of community amateur hockey, the company had never attempted to acquire an NHL franchise, something that, in my estimation, would have been costly, distracting and time-consuming.

The city of Hamilton, however, had other ideas. In the hope of attracting an NHL team, the city put up the money to build a 17,000-seat arena, Copps Coliseum, which opened in 1985. At the time, the move seemed questionable, but the city was convinced that building the arena would be a stepping stone to landing an NHL team whenever the league might decide to expand. The perception was that, with an arena in place, the city's request for a team could not be overlooked. It was a flawed notion, but the power brokers and politicians in Hamilton could not be deterred.

In 1989, when the NHL announced expansion plans, Hamilton's mayor, Bob Morrow, thought the city's moment had arrived. There was one major stumbling block: the bid lacked financial backing. The city needed an individual or group willing to put up U.S.$50 million for the franchise fee, and millions more in startup costs. It was a long shot, especially considering that there was no guarantee a franchise application would even be accepted.

Morrow was undaunted, and eventually he, along with hockey consultant Gerry Patterson, ended up in my office in Oakville. Morrow was searching for a minority stakeholder, as he felt the city already had managed to secure a majority owner for the team. Like others before him, he made the mistake of assuming I was interested in buying a stake in a hockey team. I think Morrow believed we'd be open to the idea because the company had started in Hamilton, and we had the connection to a Hall of Famer in Tim Horton.

But becoming involved with an NHL team was the furthest thing from my mind in 1990. I was in the midst of a lawsuit with Lori Horton over the ownership of the company (more on that later) and was rapidly expanding Tim Hortons. I told him politely that I wasn't the backer they were searching for.

Finding the right financier for the bid proved more difficult than Morrow expected. His majority stakeholder eventually withdrew from the project, leaving the mayor and his consultant to track down another buyer only a few months before the formal bid had to be presented to the NHL. Morrow simply wouldn't take no for an answer, even when he and Patterson came up without any viable alternatives. I received a call a few months after the initial meeting; the mayor asked if he and Patterson could come down to my office again and discuss the expansion proposal one more time. Once more I expressed my disinterest, telling Morrow he would simply be wasting his time and mine by discussing the bid with me further.

"Just give us twenty minutes," he said. Reluctantly, I agreed to meet with them once again.

Soon after arriving, Morrow and Patterson launched into the story of trying to find a backer for the team. Despite all the setbacks they had encountered, they were more persuasive in their second pitch to me. But it was also readily apparent that they were becoming frustrated by their lack of success in the face of the application deadline.

"Well, Bob, what happens if I don't become part of the bid?" I asked.

"Ron, if you don't come onside, we are out of options. There is no one else for this and it will be over. We won't be able to mount a bid."

The way he said it struck a chord with me. As opposed to our first meeting, I told Morrow to leave the matter with me to see what we could do.

Without knowing exactly how to proceed, I called the company's senior management into a meeting to consider our options. Financing would be a significant issue. How would Tim Hortons bankroll a team, let alone operate it in a way that would be in tune with the company's goals? One concept that was floated involved asking store owners to pay one percent of their advertising fees for that year, about $3.25 million—an amount that would rise as new stores opened and volumes increased—to support the team as part of a chainwide marketing initiative. We approached several key owners about the concept to see if it would meet with general support.

The other concept that was developed was to let the owners share in the purchase of the franchise by acquiring shares. This was a concept that excited many we spoke to, as the franchisees would become part of the ownership group of an NHL team, which was a dream for many of them.

The idea of using the marketing and advertising dollars from the chain seemed to gain support from the owners involved in our planning sessions. Once the idea was roughed out, it was determined that the best way to proceed would be to present it to the rest of the chain. Special regional meetings with store owners were immediately set up, and at these gatherings, the first of which was in Ontario, our idea for the team and its capitalization were presented. Both of the company's proposals received unanimous support at the meetings in Atlantic Canada and Ontario. Everyone, it seemed, wanted to have a piece of an NHL club, which came as a surprise to our management team.

We anticipated that the biggest obstacle to the idea would come from our Quebec owners, especially given the political climate in the province at the time (the Meech Lake Accord was rejected by Manitoba and Newfoundland in 1990, damaging Quebec's relationship with the "rest of Canada"). We met with our Quebec franchisees at Le Château Montebello, and were surprised, given that the proposed hockey team would be located in the heart of Ontario, that there was strong support for the plan here, as well. With the entire chain behind a bid, we convinced a couple of large financial institutions to lend us the money we would need. Going into the NHL meetings, we appeared to be the group with the soundest financing arrangement. And it looked as if there would be a real opportunity to put a deal together that would benefit both Hamilton and Tim Hortons.

The city called a hastily arranged press conference in November 1990, at which Mayor Morrow announced that Tim Hortons was prepared to become the sole backer of a bid to bring an NHL team to Hamilton. However, before we made a formal offer to the league, we needed an indication that the citizens of Hamilton would support the team by committing to buy season tickets. We set a goal of 14,000; bettering even our most optimistic estimates, 17,000 fans applied for season tickets, and there were long lineups of people eager to put down deposits on seats.

That level of support made it clear to us that Hamilton would back an NHL team if the bid was successful. It also would help our bottom line—our business plan calculated that if the team drew an average of 14,000 fans per game, Tim Hortons would see a positive return on its investment based on the information supplied to us. A survey of the fans also indicated another factor we hoped would help our bid: of all the applications for tickets, 83 percent came from the greater Hamilton area, indicating that a franchise in the city would not infringe on the ticket revenue of either the Toronto Maple Leafs or the Buffalo Sabres. This was important, because the two teams had a veto over any team being placed within a fifty-mile radius of their respective arenas. Hamilton fell into the exclusive territory of Toronto and very close to Buffalo's territory.*

As we went to the NHL's expansion meetings at the Breakers Hotel in Palm Beach, Florida, there appeared to be every reason to be optimistic that the Hamilton bid would be successful. Gerry Patterson had spoken with league president John Ziegler and been assured that a major hurdle had been cleared: the Leafs and Sabres had agreed to allow an expansion franchise to be placed in Hamilton. Patterson was told that the league's board of governors had a strong desire to see a team in Hamilton, so they had pressured the Leafs

---

* Buffalo's hold over the Hamilton market was questionable, as it depended on where one measured from. Certainly Hamilton's downtown core was outside of the geography Buffalo controlled as part of its franchise agreement.

into accepting. We were told there would have to be some indemnification payments to both clubs, but that neither Buffalo nor Toronto would stand in our way.

Despite the assurances, we were not blind to the possibility that the two cities could still pose a threat. In preparing for the meeting in Florida, I had spoken with Montreal Canadiens general manager Sam Pollock and asked his opinion on the situation. He told me that without financial consideration, the Maple Leafs would never allow a team to play in Hamilton. Pollock's comments gave us pause, but the signs coming from the NHL's head office seemed to indicate that there was a great deal of support for our bid.

We arrived in Florida during the first week of December. The owners were scheduled to meet to listen to bid presentations on the fifth and award the franchises the following day. An entourage of Tim Hortons executives and civic officials attended the meeting, but only two of us would be allowed in to make a twelve-minute presentation. Patterson and I were chosen to speak on behalf of the bid.

Given all that we had heard, we felt there was reason to be optimistic. But prior to the meeting, TDL senior vice-president Arch Jollymore and I went up to Ziegler's suite for a discussion about the bid. It did not take long for him to deflate our hopes.

"Gentlemen, you've got to come to grips with the fact there will not be a team in Hamilton," he said. We were stunned both by the rejection and by the way we were being informed of it. Nothing had prepared us for the possibility that we would be turned down, especially since we had not even had a chance to put our proposal before the governors. Ziegler continued: "You needed to settle up with Toronto and Buffalo if you had ever hoped to get a franchise. You understand that's what needed to be done, right?"

It was the first time we heard that the deal was on shaky ground, and it ran contrary to assurances Patterson and Morrow had received from the NHL earlier in the process. We had expected that we would win the board of governors' support and then negotiate with Toronto and Buffalo over indemnification.

Despite what Ziegler told us, our group remained convinced that the franchise was still a possibility. That evening, there was a social function that all of the owners were expected to attend. We continued to lobby the owners in the hope of striking a deal. We spoke with Don Giffin, who had become the president of the Maple Leafs following the death of team owner Harold Ballard. Giffin seemed to indicate that the situation over territorial exclusivity could not be resolved, but all we had heard from our lobbying efforts said it was unlikely the Leafs would risk standing in the way of Hamilton's bid. However, Seymour Knox III, the owner of the Buffalo Sabres, was a wild card. His team was struggling financially, and it became clear he might see Hamilton as siphoning off some of his team's fan support. We tried to convince both teams that great rivalries would develop between the cities and contribute to the success of all three, but our argument seemed to fall of deaf ears.

Finally, on Wednesday, we made our case to the board of governors. Our presentation included a video selling the positive aspects of Hamilton and the company's connection to Tim Horton. Then it was my turn to pitch the various owners, and I used my experience with the company to appeal to their business instincts.

"I'm in the franchise business," I told them. "We believe if you're in a market and the potential for more franchises is greater than the number you have, then you'd better move in and open a new store or someone else is going to move in and take the market away from you."

At the end of the presentation, I presented a cheque for U.S.$5 million. It was meant as a down payment on the team, with the remaining U.S.$45 million to be paid out in two separate instalments closer to the time when the team would hit the ice. I ended my presentation by saying, "Gentlemen, in my hands I hold a cheque for $5 million as a sign of good faith." Edmonton Oilers owner Peter Pocklington seemed so excited by the sight of it that it looked for an instant as if he might come over and take it from me, until Ziegler talked him out of it.

Some sports columnists said our bid had asked for terms on the franchise, but that seemed like a fair proposition to the group supporting the Hamilton bid. Otherwise we would be handing over millions of dollars to the NHL with no way to make any income on the investment while at the same time spending money to put a team together. On top of that, we would still have to negotiate with both Buffalo and Toronto for territorial rights. Perhaps it was my sense that this was a poor way to do business, but our feeling was that once the franchise was approved, we would have more negotiating sessions to work out the financial details. Interestingly, of the offers on the table, including rivals from Ottawa and Tampa, ours was the only one that had actual money prepared to back the bid. Ottawa and Tampa, which both pledged U.S.$50 million for their franchise, would still have to raise the money if their bid was successful. We felt our stronger financial terms would help us overcome any problems we faced from Buffalo and Toronto.

In many ways, and despite all the rumblings to the contrary, Hamilton was considered the leading city to acquire one of the two open franchises. Even Bruce Firestone, who was heading the Ottawa bid, approached us the night before the decision was announced to say that he felt our bid was the most likely to succeed.

The evening after we made our presentation, there were dozens of limousines in front of the hotel, waiting to take the owners and bidders to the home of Boston Bruins owner Jeremy Jacobs. As I was about to get into a car, Oilers owner Pocklington came up to tell me we had been successful—a franchise would be awarded to Hamilton.

"Hey, Ron, you've got it," he said, giving me the thumbs-up. "You might have to sweeten the terms a bit, but it is yours."

That evening at Jacobs' home, I continued to lobby the owners who were there. Our confidence was not artificial: we were convinced Hamilton had landed an NHL team.

ooooo

The following afternoon at one o'clock, the league was to disclose the names of the cities that would receive franchises. To our surprise, we learned that the groups representing Tampa and Ottawa had already spoken with the NHL about half an hour before the meeting. At one p.m., the bidders were called into a large conference room in the hotel. Ziegler stood before us all and thanked everyone for their efforts. And then, to our shock and dismay, he awarded the two available franchises to Tampa Bay and Ottawa.

Despite the backroom scuttlebutt that suggested Hamilton's bid was being undone by the power of the Toronto Maple Leafs and Buffalo Sabres, we largely failed to pay attention to the warning signs until it was too late. Tim Hortons executives and the city of Hamilton had put an immense amount of time and effort into preparing a bid on short notice, and the NHL had determined that it was preferable to reward the two bidders that had yet to actually raise the money to pay the franchise fee.

After the bid's failure, pundits suggested that Hamilton's bid failed because I had asked to pay the franchise fee over time, with an immediate down payment. To those of us on the bid team, however, our offer seemed fair, considering we would still have had to negotiate with both Buffalo and Toronto. And besides whatever indemnification we would be expected to pay, our bid would be on the hook for the considerable costs involved in starting up a team from scratch. Based on that, it seemed to me that handing over $50 million on the spot, when it would be two years before the team would even play a game (giving us a chance to realize some return on our investment), was a crazy way of doing business.

We viewed the franchise application process as a business negotiation. If you are negotiating, you don't come to the table with your best offer right away. Our hope was that, once the franchise was awarded, we would engage in further negotiations to work out the financial details. It is interesting to note that, of all the bids on the table, Hamilton's was the only one that had actual money behind it.

I was despondent at our failure. During an interview with a reporter from CHCH-TV in Hamilton, I broke down. It seemed unconscionable for it all to end as unfairly as it did. Similarly, the city was depressed by the news for weeks afterwards. Naturally, the citizens cast about to find a scapegoat, and although Tim Hortons, a company that had grown up in Hamilton, had been the sole backer of the bid, they began to turn on us and say it was Ron Joyce's fault that a franchise had not been obtained. I encountered the fallout immediately after flying back from Palm Beach. After the company jet touched down in Hamilton, a customs official boarded the plane to clear us. She asked us if we had anything to declare. I was the last person she had to speak to.

"Well, we know *you* don't have anything to declare," she said loudly.

In retrospect, the bid's failure turned out to be a saving grace. Hockey salaries exploded in the years following the bid, and most teams had trouble making ends meet as costs escalated rapidly. This resulted in the lockout that forced the cancellation of the entire 2004–05 season and led to the introduction of a salary cap. It is hard to say for certain how a Hamilton team would have fared during this tumultuous time, but my feeling is that it would have struggled.

ooooo

Soon after my return from Palm Beach, several NHL team owners contacted me to sound out my interest in buying either part or all of their franchises. I was approached by the ownership of the Pittsburgh Penguins, for example, as well as Molson Breweries, who, in addition to the Montreal Canadiens, held shares in Maple Leaf Gardens Ltd.—the parent company of the Leafs—and wanted the team to end up in the hands of someone outside the beer business. Looking back, we probably should have pursued that opportunity, although it would have put us into a battle with Steve Stavro, who was accumulating Gardens stock and finally succeeded in taking the company private in 1994. Even Seymour Knox, the owner of Buffalo who had opposed our bid, asked me whether I wanted a part of his team. I met him for a round of golf at the Hamilton Golf and Country Club in Ancaster, and during our time on the links, I asked him about the chances that Hamilton might still get an NHL franchise. He said that with the Buffalo franchise already struggling financially, he simply could not afford to lose fans to Hamilton from cities like St. Catharines on the Canadian side of the border.

"Ron, there will never be a team in Hamilton as long as I'm alive," he said. "That's all there is to it."

One of the negative side effects of TDL's bid for an NHL franchise was that our whole management team had been focused on the bid;

consequently, we took our eye off of the business we were in. It was an issue we would set out to resolve when management was called together after the bid's failure to determine how the company should go forward. A positive aspect was all of the publicity we had received for the brand. This resulted in large sales increases and increased awareness.

ooooo

The Hamilton NHL bid would not be my last dalliance with professional hockey, although perhaps it should have been.

I was invited to the All-Star Game in Montreal in 1993 and met with people from the Calgary Flames. A group of owners involved with the team, including the Seaman brothers, Doc and B.J., and Harley Hotchkiss, asked whether I had any interest in purchasing the entire franchise. It appeared that the group that controlled the Flames was concerned with rising salary costs and had been looking for a way to divest themselves of the team since their Stanley Cup win in 1989. Calgary was a small market, one in which it was becoming difficult to operate. The expansion had established the value of an NHL franchise at U.S.$50 million, many times the amount the group had paid for the team when it moved from Atlanta in 1980. The time seemed right to seek a buyer, and they hoped Tim Hortons might put forward an offer similar to the one we had made in 1990.

The idea did not really resonate with me, but I brought the Tim Hortons executive team to Calgary to see if we might make the idea work. We came away unimpressed, since the numbers did not indicate that the business would be strong; we decided not to acquire the Flames. It didn't take long for the owners to dream up another concept—selling minority stakes in the team. They decided to bring in six new partners at various levels. Murray Edwards and I became equal partners with Harley, Doc and B.J. at 15.1 percent. The remaining partners—Grant Bartlett, Bud McCaig, Al Markin and Al Libin—split the balance equally between them. Two members of the syndicate, Norman Kwong and Sonia Scurfield, were bought out, and money was invested in improvements to the Saddledome, the arena where the Flames played.

Owning a smaller stake would prove less risky, but would also offer less benefit to Tim Hortons. Actually, the concept didn't hold out a lot of appeal at first, and we stalled for quite a while before coming to a decision. Finally, Hotchkiss called, asking very directly whether I was in or out.

Having flirted with purchasing a team for several years, I finally decided to become part of one. I felt it was a way of being a meaningful part of the community in Calgary, where I had purchased a home a few years before, and it would be interesting to be involved in a business venture with such legends as the Seaman family. The ownership changes were announced at the end of October 1994, more than a year after I had first been approached about acquiring the whole team.

While much would later be made of my unhappiness about the way the team was managed and its financial performance, it was enjoyable at the start. It was exciting to be around the players again, so many years after I had spent time with Tim and the Maple Leafs. But the rapport between the players and owners had changed, especially since agents and contracts really kept the two sides from trusting one another. Despite that I got to know a handful of players, largely through social events, and remained in touch with some of them.

The Calgary ownership, which was made up largely of entrepreneurs and businessmen from Alberta, also proved to be a challenge.

Specifically, Hotchkiss was more involved in the team's management than I thought was appropriate. He enjoyed a great deal of goodwill because he had secured the franchise for Calgary, and consequently he often didn't treat the other partners as his equals. He had the best seat in the owners' box, for example, which, petty as it seems, could lead to conflict. There was an occasion when I sat in a seat in the owners' box, only to have Murray Edwards pull me aside.

"That's Harley's seat," he told me.

"I didn't know the owners' box came with reserved seats," I replied, not moving from my spot. The issue reached another level when the Saddledome was renovated, and Hotchkiss wanted the seats in the new owners' box to be assigned. It seemed like a strange notion, since most of the owners gave the best seats in the box to their guests.

By the mid-1990s it also became clear that the sliding Canadian dollar and rising player salaries would put a lot of pressure on the team's bottom line. Rather than simply being able to enjoy owning part of a hockey team, we had to regularly inject additional money into the team to keep it afloat. By 2001, seven years after I acquired the stake in the franchise, I had grown tired of all of the financial and operating problems facing the team, so I sold my stake in the Flames to the existing owners.

With my role at Tim Hortons changing, and my stake in the Flames divested, I was ready to embark on a new chapter in my life.

13

DONUT WAR

For several years after I purchased Tim's stake in Tim Hortons from her, Lori Horton remained peripherally involved with the company. Specifically, she continued as the president of the Tim Horton Memorial Camp in Parry Sound, and she often travelled with me to new store openings through much of the late 1970s.

In truth, we had a social relationship that lasted well beyond the sale of her stake in the chain. We often dated and went to dinners, parties and Tim Hortons events together. Though she would later publicly say we did not get along following the death of Tim in 1974, in reality we spent far more time together in the years after his accident than we had before it.

However, her relationship with the chain, and with me personally, began to deteriorate in the early 1980s. Though her financial position was not entirely clear, it was becoming apparent the money she had received from the sale of her family's stake in the chain, a total of

$1 million, was starting to dwindle. That was quite surprising, considering that it had been set up to make her comfortable for life.

Six years after I bought her shares, I recall being at the office with Lori and Mel Rothwell, who had been the company's financial adviser in the early days, and who had continued to work with Lori after the sale. It became clear from her behaviour that there was something seriously wrong with her, and we asked if she was ill. She was slurring her words, and some of the things she said didn't make sense.

"Lori, are you on drugs?" I eventually asked. "There's something unusual about you."

She showed us a large bottle of pills of various sizes and colours. She said that they were just vitamins and medications. I asked if I could have one of each, and she agreed. We then went for dinner, and afterwards she asked for the pills back because it would leave her short. I had left them at the office and it was too far to go back, so we agreed that I would mail them to her. I contacted a friend of mine who was able to identify exactly what they were. To put it simply, they were not substances that were in her best interest.

There had long been rumours of substance abuse, but I never knew for certain whether the speculation and innuendo was true. Tim never shared his marital or personal difficulties with me, and though I knew Lori had been hospitalized a couple of times, no reason was given for her medical issues, nor was one expected.

In the years after her sale of the family's stake in the company, Tim Hortons had successfully broken ground in Atlantic Canada and was making significant inroads into the west. The chain, which had forty-eight restaurants when Lori sold her stake on December 23, 1975, was five times the size a decade later. The chain had succeeded beyond our wildest dreams, but it had come about through the hard work of the company's executive team and its store owners. Nothing happened by chance.

My relationship with Lori did deteriorate, but not in the time frame she would later suggest. In fact, sometime around the tenth anniversary of the opening of the Tim Horton Memorial Camp in Parry Sound, it appeared that she started to listen to people around her who said she had been taken advantage of when she sold her interest in Tim Hortons to me. Among those who had significant influence over Lori were Eddie and Norma Shack, who continually told her she had been coerced into agreeing to an unfair deal.

It was an awkward situation, since I had known Eddie for many years and was aware that sometimes he could make rash, unreasonable sounding comments in public. Though Eddie was pushing Lori to launch a lawsuit, he was still friendly to my face. According to a former teammate of Tim's who appeared at the anniversary event, during the celebration there was even some open discussion among the Shacks and Lori about launching legal action over the sale of her shares. In the end, it is unclear how much sway the Shacks had over Lori's decisions, but other events that occurred through the middle of the 1980s eventually pushed her to take rash action against the TDL group.

As I mentioned earlier, in 1986 work began on a second camp, to be opened near my hometown of Tatamagouche, Nova Scotia. The camp was not my idea; it was conceived by Gary O'Neill, who had opened the first store in Moncton in the months following Tim's death. But once I became convinced of the potential of a camp in Atlantic Canada, we moved forward quickly.

After we became convinced of the merits of a second facility, we decided we should approach Lori, who remained as president of the Memorial Camp in Parry Sound. However, once the subject was broached, she immediately became hostile towards the idea. She could not be convinced to change her position, even when it was made clear to her the Parry Sound operation would be the only camp to memorialize Tim.

"I'm not going to approve the camp," she told me when we informed her we were going ahead with the second children's camp.

I asked her why she'd stand in the way.

"Well, you didn't consult with me and I'm the president of the foundation," she said.

"Look, Lori, there's only one memorial camp to Tim," she was told. "This is a camp for underprivileged children and has nothing to do with the first camp. If you don't want to stay on as president of the overall children's foundation, we'll leave you as the president of the Memorial Camp and we'll make the camp in Tatamagouche distinct from the one in Parry Sound."

By this time, the proceeds from the sale of the chain in 1975 had largely disappeared. Once flush with money well invested for a good income, two expensive homes and a new car, by 1983, according to statements she would later make in court, all that was left was $19,000.

When we went to Tatamagouche for the sod-turning ceremony in 1987, Lori did not attend in an official capacity. Instead, she was introduced as the widow of the company's co-founder. Though she had said she wasn't interested in being involved in a second camp, she apparently viewed her exclusion as a slight and was offended by not being asked to participate.

Dick Trainor, who was a director of the foundation and a long-time friend, flew home with Lori following the opening ceremonies. Unhappy and feeling snubbed, Lori made statements to the effect that a lawsuit was going to proceed. From that point, it was clearly in my best interest to distance myself from her. Lori was told she would always be welcome at Tim Horton Memorial Camp, but she decided to step down from her position as president of the foundation.

I'm sure there were people who felt sorry for Lori. In some ways it is understandable. For much of her life, she had the wealth and prestige of being the spouse of one of hockey's most famous and beloved players, as well as a woman who was widowed by a terrible accident. But the wealth and prestige diminished in time, and I think she began to feel ostracized from the franchises that sported her husband's name. The truth was that she had been well paid in a business deal that could have potentially backfired on me. But she had few money-management skills and could not look after the rewards she received for selling her portion of TDL.

After several years of rumours, Lori finally launched her legal challenge of the sale of the Horton interest in the chain in December 1987. Her demands were quite clear: she wanted half of TDL, and $10 million for money she had lost over the previous decade. Lori was planning to argue to the court that she had been incompetent at the time of the sale, due to drug and alcohol abuse that left her too impaired to make the decision to sell her interest in Tim Hortons. She also named her lawyer, Jim Blaney, in the suit, alleging that he had conspired with me to take advantage of her impairment. It was a remarkable twist, considering that it had been Blaney who requested that Lori receive an additional $150,000 for Tim Hortons when the sale was negotiated in 1975. She also stated that she did not receive fair value for her shares, and asked to be reinstated as an officer and director of Tim Donut Ltd.

When the lawsuit finally landed, I was not surprised. Lori and I had enough friends in common that I could be sure it was going to become a reality. But seeing it coming didn't make it any less disappointing. I knew that, regardless of the outcome, people who were uninformed of the details of the sale might side with Lori. And the court case would almost certainly hurt my reputation and standing in the Canadian business community among those who only followed the proceedings casually. When I became involved in the first stores, the company had no real value at all. Eight years after Tim and I became partners, we had enhanced the value from zero to $1 million for her benefit.

It may have been a strong deal at the time, but the hard work and dedication of the TDL team over the ensuing decade had increased the chain's value tremendously and made Tim Hortons a great success story in the Canadian food-service industry. Understand, however, that this was no accident; it isn't as if someone sprinkled stardust on the company and it magically grew. It was because of the ingenuity and labour of a lot of very dedicated people who bought into the philosophy that had made Tim Hortons and who were willing to take calculated risks that paid off over time. The company's accomplishments in the decade after acquiring Lori's shares were achieved because we were more focused on the basic fundamentals of our business than our competition was. Because of that, I didn't feel Lori had a valid claim on any of the proceeds beyond 1975.

I remained convinced that Lori had been treated more than fairly in the sale of her portion of the business, and I believed strongly that the case should never have made it to court. In our negotiations, Lori had been represented by one of the top law firms in the country, and she was treated honourably by everyone involved. Given the agreement between Tim and me, which clearly placed me in control of the company after his death, I could have acted as the majority partner and forced her to acquiesce as far as the company was concerned. She could have been fired as a company executive or shuffled to the side. Some have argued that it would have been better to have made her a silent partner, though I'm not sure how successful that would have been. Instead, I tried to find a place for her in the business. When that failed, I purchased her stake in the company for an amount that exceeded even independent estimates. The contract had been visible and she was well informed on every aspect of it. It was a fair and equitable deal, and Lori was treated with respect and allowed to maintain a relationship with the company following the sale. In retrospect, the 1975 deal was fair and generous. Lori was not interested in the business, and in fact, wanted to be free of it. The money she received was more than the value provided by two independent appraisers.

Five years after the case was started, it finally found its way before a judge. Starting in October 1992 and lasting for three months, friends and associates, including my ex-wife Teri, paraded in and out of the witness box, testifying about Lori's state of mind during the years after Tim's death. The whole time, I sat in the courtroom and was instructed to remain detached from the proceedings, regardless of how embarrassing or untrue some of the testimony might be.

Lori's case relied upon having witnesses argue she had been too influenced by alcohol and prescription medication to fully comprehend the sale of Tim Hortons. Most of the evidence had little to do with me. While I was disgusted with the whole tawdry affair, it must have been very difficult and embarrassing for Lori to hear tales told in open court about how she had been so at a loss of her faculties that she had been carried out of people's homes.

While it may have been true that Lori had substance abuse problems, I was never aware of them and they certainly never affected her decisions during the time she worked as a partner at Tim Hortons.

Long after the sale, when I would meet her at the camp in Parry Sound, it became apparent to me that she had some personal problems, but this would have been years after the sale of the company, and not in the months following Tim's death as she alleged in her suit.

Losing the case would likely have meant the end of Tim Hortons as it existed at the time. To give Lori the damages she was seeking would have bankrupted the company. I'd been advised by my friend, Dick Trainor, then a Canadian judge, that the legal system was not always predictable. He suggested that we seek a settlement, and my lawyer, Earl Cherniak, came to the same conclusion.

"Ron, I don't think you can lose this case, but it can drag on for years," Earl told me. "It isn't something you want hanging over you. I'm obligated to advise you to try to find an offer that will make this go away."

The notion of settling, especially after my reputation had been sullied by the insinuations made in the case, was difficult to accept. But in the end, we agreed to offer Lori a settlement that included a car and a salary of $100,000. It would make Lori financially secure for the rest of her life—again.

Though it was never quite clear why, Lori's lawyer, John Ritchie, appeared to feel the case had merit and might be won. For her part, Lori viewed the offer as a sign of weakness and an indication that her case was strong. She flatly declined to take the deal.

Despite our best efforts, the judge determined that the case should go forward, and my legal team spent several years interviewing witnesses and preparing my defence. Once the case went forward in October 1992, Earl introduced a motion for summary judgment, meaning that the lawyers argue their respective cases relying solely on affidavit evidence—no witnesses would testify. However, the motion was turned down by Madam Justice Patricia German, meaning that a trial would ensue and witnesses for both sides would give evidence to the courts in a process that would end up taking months.

Lori was the first witness called in the case. My lawyer had felt she would not be a strong witness, and he was correct: she contradicted herself, making comments that ran contrary to her discovery. Under Earl's cross-examination, Lori appeared to admit that her relationship with me was not quite as she characterized it in her earlier testimony, and she added that she had been actively involved with the foundation well after Tim's death and the sale of TDL. She seemed unprepared for the level of scrutiny she was placed under at the trial, and her case started to unravel right from the start.

Her supporting witnesses, who included Norma Shack, among others, were not particularly convincing, either. Repeatedly, Earl Cherniak and Paul Bates, the other lawyer representing me, asked witnesses for Lori's side about her problems with medication and alcohol and to pinpoint when these problems arose. Many questions revolved around the timeline Lori was presenting. We didn't dispute whether she had a problem, but when the problem occurred. Witnesses were also asked why, if her condition was as grave as they were suggesting, they did not step in to help Lori in 1975.

In my opinion, much of the testimony greatly exaggerated the true circumstances. George McGlinchey, one of the earliest Tim Hortons franchise owners, testified on Lori's behalf, which led me to ask him about it later over lunch. It angered me that several of Lori's key witnesses were friends of mine who were not clearly remembering the timing of her problems.

I think George just had his dates mixed up. Everything he recounted happened after the sale. There was no question she had issues with drugs after the sale, but that fact was far from clear prior to my acquisition of the company.

Midway through the trial, the courts decided to try and settle by mediation. Mr. Justice Douglas Lissaman spoke to us and tried to propose a settlement. I was reluctant but we agreed, and a very generous offer was put forth, one that included a salary with an annual increase based on inflation, an expense account and a car. Justice Lissaman presented the offer to Lori and her lawyer, then reported to us that it had been rejected. I still can't believe that it seemed we were put in a position of having to make the offer in the first place, because it seemed unfair. I guess we were fortunate that it was rejected.

I was called as the first defence witness, and I spent three days in the box recounting the history of TDL and Tim Hortons, how the company had evolved and Lori's role in it following Tim's accident. It was a very stressful time for me as I was continuing to run TDL, while also attending and testifying at the trial. My testimony began on a Thursday, and partway through my testimony on Friday, I came down with the flu, surely heightened by the stress of the trial. Partially recovered, I concluded my time on the stand on Monday.

Though the case wrapped up in December, it took until February to receive a ruling from Justice German. When it came to dismissing Lori's case against everybody she sued, it was devastating for Lori, as it rejected most of her arguments.

Justice German wrote, "It must be remembered that it would not be proper to look at the success of TDL today and assume that [it] was a known fact in 1975." It was an interesting and insightful comment. After all, if Tim Hortons had failed in the early 1980s when our debts were high and interest rates rose dramatically, there can be little doubt that Lori would have told people she had received great value for her stake in the business and dodged a bullet.

"The plaintiff has put forward a remarkable position in this lawsuit," the judge continued. "Mrs. Horton claims that for almost twenty years she consumed amphetamines and alcohol to such an extent she lacked the mental capacity to make a financial decision . . . although during the period she admits she had the mental capacity to, amongst other things, drive a car, attend an office, travel, be an executrix of her husband's will, attend numerous social and business functions where she was in the public eye and to be a director of a foundation."

The ruling called much of Lori's testimony into question. "Her memory, or lack of it, seems to be convenient," the judge said, while noting that Lori's decision to sell her share in Tim Hortons "involved selling the major asset of Mr. Horton's estate, but I believe, as I stated, Mrs. Horton was well aware of this fact because, for one reason, she considered her decision for some time."

The major hurdle that Lori's case could not overcome was that her witnesses had simply not proven she was incompetent at the time of the sale. "I am satisfied that Mr. Joyce dealt fairly, reasonably and honestly with Mrs. Horton," Justice German wrote, adding, "There was no evidence which would satisfy me on the balance of probabilities that Mr. Joyce could have known she was mentally incompetent and I am satisfied the transaction was fair and reasonable to Mrs. Horton."

The conclusion of the case was a vindication for me, as it confirmed that the sale had been fair and that it had been a mutual agreement that led to my acquisition of the Horton stake in the business. It was a deal that allowed Tim Hortons to be expanded into the outstanding company that it became. For me, the sale had never been about the money; it was about the opportunity to realize the chain's full potential.

The other factor that was never taken into account during the case was its potential impact on Tim Hortons' store owners. By 1992, there were 650 franchisees who had invested their savings and put their energy and time into running a business. Those individuals had nothing to do with the sale of the company in 1975 and were always innocent of any wrongdoing towards Mrs. Horton. Unfortunately for them, the case put the spotlight on the entire company, including the franchise owners. It placed a negative connotation on the Tim Hortons name for some time, and this was unfair to those who had helped build the chain.

Of course, there are still people who feel Lori didn't get what she deserved when she sold the company in 1975, but their opinions are based more on emotion than on law or fact. Many think of Lori as the "poor widow," but there was nothing poor about Lori. She was a smart woman who had little ability to deal with money and who lost her life savings in a deliberate manner that lacked any foresight. When she cashed the cheque for $1 million on December 23, 1975, she seemed like the happiest, most gregarious person in the world. She was a rich woman and we were both happy with the deal. It should have ended there.

I'm often asked why there is no memorabilia of Tim Horton in the stores. Shortly after Tim's death in 1974, I commissioned a portrait to be painted by a well-known Toronto artist, featuring Tim in his Buffalo Sabres uniform. We had prints made of the painting and they were distributed throughout the system, and placed in every store. In the 1990s, Don Schroeder felt that it was time to have a more recent portrait for the stores, so he commissioned artist Ken Danby to create an updated painting of Tim. At the time, I was reluctant to proceed given the ongoing legal problems involving Lori Horton, but I would later agree. I purchased the painting from Ken with the idea that we would create 100 signed proofs of the original and then sell them with the proceeds to be shared between Ken and the Tim Horton Children's Foundation.

Soon after the prints started appearing in the stores, Lori began a $1-million lawsuit against the company and me, claiming the wrongful use of Tim's image. As a compromise, we contacted her lawyers and offered to remove the offending prints from the stores and to stop selling them. It was disappointing that it had come to that since we had full legal rights to the use of his image. Lori proceeded with the lawsuit and, rightly so, it was dismissed with no cause of action. That finally ended all litigation by Lori against me and TDL.

Lori must still have held out hope that the case was salvageable, because she launched an appeal. In 1995 a judge ruled that the courts would not hear the case. Her attempt to get back the company she had sold had failed.

After the case was finished, Lori approached me through one of her daughters for a meeting. It was hard for me to do after all the hostilities that had arisen in the five years during which the case had been fought. But we shared a grandchild (my son Ron Jr. had married Jeri-Lyn Horton, and they currently operate a Tim Hortons store). As it turned out, we never did get the chance to really talk after the end of the lawsuit. We would see each other at family gatherings. It wasn't unpleasant; there just wasn't anything to talk about.

Lori died suddenly in December 2000. Soon after, my son Ron called to talk about the funeral, and it was decided that TDL would assume all costs associated with this. In recent years, I made a financial commitment to Tim and Lori's daughters. Each year, a tax-free sum is allotted to Kim, Kelly and Tracy to enhance their current lifestyle.

It had taken seven years for the case to fully run its course, a period in which Tim Hortons had been witness to massive growth and success. In many ways, 1995 would prove to be one of the pivotal points in the company's history.

Some of the selection of cream products we made in the early years. I insisted that the products were always fresh. It was the only way to keep our customers happy and be sure they would return.

We opened our first distribution warehouse in Oakville in 1971. We used branded packaging, as is seen in this photo, on all of the products that were sent across the country.

We rarely raised the prices of our coffee and donuts in the formative years of the company. Donuts cost a dime a piece when I purchased the first store, or 69 cents a dozen. In the late 1960s, the price of a donut rose to 15 cents.

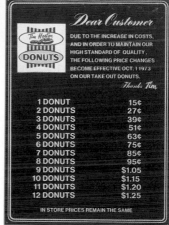

Dear Customer

DUE TO THE INCREASE IN COSTS, AND IN ORDER TO MAINTAIN OUR HIGH STANDARD OF QUALITY, THE FOLLOWING PRICE CHANGES BECOME EFFECTIVE OCT. 1 1973 ON OUR TAKE OUT DONUTS.

Thanks Tim

1 DONUT	15¢
2 DONUTS	27¢
3 DONUTS	39¢
4 DONUTS	51¢
5 DONUTS	63¢
6 DONUTS	75¢
7 DONUTS	85¢
8 DONUTS	95¢
9 DONUTS	$1.05
10 DONUTS	$1.15
11 DONUTS	$1.20
12 DONUTS	$1.25

IN STORE PRICES REMAIN THE SAME

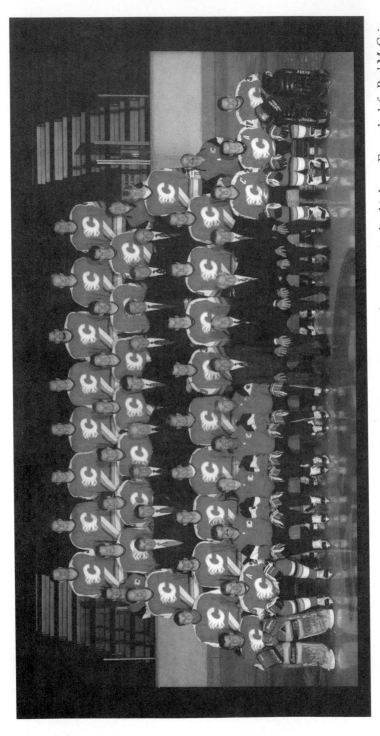

In October 1994, I purchased a stake in the Calgary Flames. The team's group of owners are in the third row. From the left: Bud McCaig, Grant Bartlett, me, Harley Hotchkiss, Murray Edwards, Doc Seaman, Allan Markin, Al Libin and B.J. Seaman.

In our haste to get the kids camp concept off the ground, we acquired an old, unreliable bus. We soon replaced the bus with one that could be counted on to get the children to Parry Sound.

The Tim Hortons Children's Foundation now includes six camps in Canada and the U.S. This photo, taken at the 1994 opening of our fourth camp in Quyon, Quebec, shows just how many people played pivotal roles in helping establish each and every facility. From left to right: David Sobey, John Cassaday, Don Schroeder, Frank Cella, Michele Thornley, Gary O'Neill, Bill Fitz, John Hoey, Gov. General Ray Hnatyshyn, me, Dick Trainor, Jean Pigott, Drew McCaughey, Wayne Newson, Tony Eames and Dale Jollymore.

I've also had the good fortune to meet several presidents, including George H.W. Bush, Jimmy Carter and Bill Clinton, pictured here in 2004 at a visit to Fox Harb'r along with former U.S. ambassadors to Canada James Blanchard, on the left, and Gordon Giffin.

Celine Dion sitting with my mother, Grace, at our national conference held in Ottawa in 1994. My son Grant is on my right, and Lynn Kilgore is on the left.

Though she had her share of struggles in early years, my mother is an astounding testament to perseverance. She turned 95 in 2006 and is still vibrant. Here, she and I cut the cake at the sod-turning ceremony for the children's ranch at Kananaskis in July 1990.

After I sold Tim Hortons to Wendy's, I pursued several of my passions, including sailing. In October 2002 we launched *Destination Fox Harb'r* in Auckland, New Zealand.

I've spent a lot of time over the past few years at my resort, Fox Harb'r, in Nova Scotia, after the sale of TDL, enjoying life, including time spent fishing, hunting and golfing.

14

RRRRROLLING UP THE SALES

As the 1980s drew to a close, TDL found itself in a position to take Tim Hortons to unprecedented heights. The fact that debt was very much under control meant that funds could be devoted to expansion, and we kicked into overdrive. All the factors that had made Tim Hortons successful in its first two decades contributed even more to the growth of the company. Our real-estate strategy, developed in the early years, had become a significant revenue stream for the company. With more stores came the demand for more supplies, all of which were sold through our distribution system. What had started out so simply had become a runaway business success. We added thirty-nine stores to the chain in 1989, and doubled that number in 1990, when we hit a milestone and added our 500th store. At this point, the company was doubling in size every five years.

We were also establishing one of our most enduring promotions. In 1985, Roger Wilson at Lily Cup approached the company about an idea they had developed. Wilson would regularly call on our management; at the time, Tim Hortons had two cup suppliers, and Lily was trying to gain a larger share of our business, which would be especially lucrative for the firm, given our growth rate at the time.

On this particular day, Wilson was stopping by to demonstrate a new cup his company had developed, one which allowed for a message to be printed under the rim, making it ideal for some sort of contest. Since no one had attempted such a thing in Canada to that date, the concept was attractive.

Ron Buist, who was managing Tim Hortons' marketing department at the time, was assigned to come up with a way of using the cups in a promotional campaign. He developed the "Roll Up the Rim" idea, and in February 1986 the campaign made its debut. At first, the prizes were simple: Tim Hortons coffee and other products. People loved the concept, and it didn't take us long to realize it was a great way to promote coffee sales in the spring, when they traditionally languished. There was a slight rise in sales when we ran the campaign in 1986, but it was much bigger a year later. By 1988, we were also giving away automobiles. The contest really captured the Canadian public's imagination, and every year sales would surge during the run of the Roll Up the Rim promotion.

Our main problem, especially at first, was gauging the popularity of the promotion and figuring out how many cups to order. If we planned too cautiously, of course, we would run out of cups, leaving customers unhappy. That actually happened a few times in early years, often a week or two before the promotion was supposed to end. Of course, we'd order significantly more the next year, only to send many of them to a landfill when they weren't used. Getting the numbers right was always more of an art than a science, and required a degree of guesswork.

I think what really put the promotion over the top was the decision in the 1990s to use an actor in our radio and television commercials who spoke with a thick Scottish burr, advising customers that it was time again to "r-r-r-roll up the r-r-r-rim to win." It made the tagline that much catchier. As of this writing, Tim Hortons has literally used billions of cups in the promotion.

ooooo

By the late 1980s, my management team at TDL had begun to evolve. Long-time TDL executive Arch Jollymore had risen to senior vice-president, while Henry Svazas, who had long been involved in scouting and making astute real-estate transactions for the company, was also given the title of vice-president. Paul House, who had started with the company as vice-president of marketing, was appointed executive vice-president of operations in 1990, while Alf Lane was vice-president in charge of real estate and legal affairs.

During this time, I began delegating many of the day-to-day managerial tasks. I still carried out my work as president and sole owner, and had to approve all expenditures, but we had very capable people in place to run the operation effectively. One of our fundamental requirements when we hired new executives was that they had to be capable of working independently. I still paid careful attention to strategic issues, but the new management structure allowed me a bit more time for life outside of work for the first time since I was twelve.

It was during this time that the company's focus on operations helped bring a degree of consistency to the new franchises we were opening. We launched an "Always Fresh" campaign that presented monetary awards to store owners if they met or exceeded the business's standards. Keeping stores in line with expectations is always a challenge in any franchise operation, and I'm proud of the fact that by this time less than 5 percent of our restaurants had any trouble meeting company standards.

Over the years, I believed that everyone involved in the company had worked to create an environment that focused on "we" instead of "I." Therefore, in December 2005, when *Maclean's* magazine featured a small blurb about Paul House in an article entitled "Newsmakers—winners," I objected to the distorted view it presented of Tim Hortons and its development. The article said House had "turned a dumpy chain of 200 doughnut shops into the best food-service brand in Canada." I felt these comments did a disservice to all of those who worked over four decades to build the company. House became chief operating officer of TDL in 1995, when we already had more than 1,200 stores in the chain, and those stores were operating at peak efficiency with a mission to present a clean and fresh environment for our customers.

Though raising standards across the chain was always our aim, TDL had long been interested in progressive business moves that would benefit the restaurants. Among the ideas floated among senior staff was the idea to make the company's restaurants smoke-free, a controversial concept that was certainly ahead of its time. Smoking had always been an issue in our restaurants, as the smell of cigarettes would end up in the products that were on display to be sold, diminishing their flavour. Some would argue that committed smokers were the chain's best customers, but it had always been my feeling that the smoke-filled environment in some of our stores actually discouraged non-smokers from entering them. While the idea of smoke-free restaurants has become commonplace in Canada, and has even been legislated in many locales, the concept was considered revolutionary in the early 1980s when we first began to consider it.

One of the major issues with the idea was that our stores had effectively become social centres in many towns and cities; people would come and sip their coffee while smoking. To remedy the problem, we spent millions trying to clean the air with a variety of air-filtering systems, but we could never find a satisfactory solution. I finally concluded that it was time to go non-smoking. At our company convention in 1984 in Fort Lauderdale, Florida, I advocated the idea of starting to eliminate smoking from our stores. As a test, we decided to make two locations 100 percent smoke-free. The first was at Main and Wellington streets in Hamilton, and then Len Graham opened the second one in Kitchener. There was a lot of resistance to the idea. I recall entering the new training centre in Oakville soon after the policy was instituted, only to find one of the customers attempting to hold a cigarette out of view while standing in line. I quietly walked up behind him.

"Pardon me," I said. "I'm afraid you might burn my non-smoking sign with your cigarette."

"Touché," he responded, stubbing out the offending smoke.

The majority of our store owners rejected the idea of non-smoking stores, with the exception of Danny Murphy, who owned several in Charlottetown. He agreed to make them non-smoking, but the move backfired badly and his sales plummeted by 30 percent in a short period of time. After a month, we agreed to reinstate smoking in his stores, and to help his case, I took out a full-page ad in the Charlottetown *Guardian* apologizing to his customers for the attempt to go non-smoking and assuring them it was a corporate initiative. His sales soon returned to normal—there was even a slight increase. But the seeds had been sown, and as the world became more aware of the health concerns related to smoking, we began making inroads. As the idea gained popularity, I decided to build separate smoking rooms in our restaurants, outfitting them with their own air-circulation systems that vented them separately.

It took years, and we did encounter additional resistance in provinces such as Newfoundland and Quebec, but these changes never go easily. The chain is now entirely smoke-free.

ooooo

Our entry into drive-thru windows started with a closed Church's Chicken franchise in Hamilton on Upper Gage and Fennell avenues. I was not a fan of them because they detracted from our large displays of products on back shelves and in showcases. When customers entered our stores, the sights and smells of freshly made products was a sure trigger for impulse buying. A drive-thru window takes all that away. The issues for chicken, hamburger and pizza stores are not nearly the same, because most of their customers know what they want. These stores also use different ways of prompting impulse purchases that don't involve displays.

Paul House had very strong opinions about the potential for drive-thrus based on the success of other chains. I never questioned whether they would work, because they obviously do, and they are very popular with store owners, because they account for a significant portion of revenue. I just wasn't sure they were the right vehicle for our chain, and in my opinion they have dramatically changed the way we conduct our business today.

Despite my hesitation, owners increasingly demanded drive-thru lanes after our first experiments proved successful. Today, even if fuel prices are at all-time highs, people still line up in their cars in large numbers to use drive-thrus. From the very start, the argument against drive-thru lanes was that they would make coffee account for a disproportionate part of our revenue. And that is exactly what happened. Anyone in business will tell you it's unwise to depend on a single product; diversification is a virtue. If, for any reason, there was an unforeseen development—say, a health scare involving coffee—it could have a hugely detrimental impact. And it is interesting to note that, even after the introduction of drive-thrus, some of the highest-volume stores in the Tim Hortons system were the restaurants that did not offer the service.

Though it took me some time to warm to the idea that drive-thrus were the way of the future, once we adopted them, I began thinking about ways to maximize their potential. In Florida in the 1980s, I had observed a new phenomenon at certain hamburger restaurants: double drive-thrus. Several chains did significant volumes by offering little more than a spot to pull up your car and place an order. There was no inside seating, and because of the lower labour and occupancy costs, they could deliver product to the marketplace more cheaply than Burger King, Wendy's and McDonald's. I was fascinated with the idea and decided we should develop double drive-thrus for Tim Hortons: drive-thrus with multiple windows, like you see at service stations, or at certain banks. We even imagined drive-thrus with four windows, though that never came to fruition.

An in-house design by Mike Wendelaar was created for the double-drive-thru concept, and we opened an experimental outlet at a mall located south of our head office in Oakville, on the west side of Dorval Drive. The theory was not to discount our products, but to maintain the same pricing found in all of the stores, which would offer a strong margin to the operators of these franchises. In time, the double drive-thru became a huge success, doing large volumes with a significantly lower cost structure. I then approached John Lacey, CEO and chairman of Scott's Hospitality, which had several locations at service centres along Highways 400 and 401 leading out of Toronto, and asked them to consider building a double drive-thru at the gas pumps on the northbound side of the 400. They were reluctant to do so. To alleviate their concerns, I offered to assume all of the costs associated with the building and equipment. They would service it from their full-service store in the food court and operate the drive-thru in exchange for TDL receiving 30 percent of gross sales as a rental charge.

"You are going to see a great return on this one," I told them, but they remained unconvinced, so TDL agreed to put up the costs associated with the double drive-thru. The concept was a resounding success, so much so that Scott's wanted to buy it back from us six months after it opened, and we agreed. Remarkably, the drive-thru did not affect the in-store sales of the existing conventional Tim Hortons on the site.

ooooo

Drive-thrus were not the only change to the business landscape during this period. The face of Tim Hortons' competition changed as well, as new players like Coffee Time, Robin's Donuts, Mister C's, Baker's Dozen Donuts and many others entered the market. The problem was that most of these rivals were more interested in selling franchises than in satisfying customers. They also had to deal with Tim Hortons, which was dominating many markets at this time. With 400 locations spread across the country, TDL had a number of advantages over its competitors. Because of our distribution system and buying power, our franchisees were able to get the supplies they needed at significantly lower prices. And we could hedge the price of coffee to deal with price fluctuations. Our marketing dollars allowed us to reinforce the Tim Hortons brand in ways that smaller or less established companies could only hope to.

However, as new donut companies evolved, a long-time competitor in Quebec, Dunkin' Donuts, began to fade away. By the 1980s, the Rosenberg family had sold off much of its interest in Dunkin' Donuts, and that left the company, which was the largest donut and coffee operation in the world at the time, ripe for a $305 million hostile takeover that came in 1989 from George Mann's Kingsbridge Capital Group, with backing from Bernie Syron, the former chairman of Cara Foods.

The situation caught Bob Rosenberg, the chair of Dunkin' Donuts, off guard. He would even accuse me of being involved in the takeover, as I had owned some Dunkin' Donuts shares during the same period and Syron was a close associate. But I had no prior knowledge of Kingsbridge's or Cara's attempt.

I spoke with Bob, whom I considered a friend, and let him know that I would not become involved in a hostile takeover against him.

"Well, Ron, Bernie Syron is a friend of mine and he is involved. We've had meetings for years and now he's stabbed me in the back," Rosenberg replied. I guess it seemed like it to him.

In order to fend off the takeover, Rosenberg was forced to look for a white knight and found one in Allied Lyons PLC. Allied Lyons was very interested in Dunkin' Donuts because it also owned a donut mix plant, and the prospect of coupling it with a business that used their products was an attractive one.

In the end, Allied Lyons offered $25 million more for Dunkin' Donuts than the bid by Mann and Syron, and it won the takeover fight. Allied Lyons also owned the Baskin-Robbins ice cream chain and they married the two brands in some instances, providing stores where both were offered. Because it wasn't the parent company's sole focus, Dunkin' Donuts suffered, though it remained an important brand in the U.S. and other parts of the world. In late 2005, Dunkin' Donuts would undergo another upheaval, being sold by Pernod Ricard (which had earlier acquired Allied Lyons) to a group of three large investment firms.

Of course, Dunkin' Donuts was not the only company that was attracting suitors in the late 1980s. Allied Lyons had also entered into negotiations about purchasing TDL around the same time. Overtures were also made by Scott's Hospitality and by John Bitove Sr., who ran several franchise operations. But far from looking for a buyer, TDL was focused specifically on growth. The aim was to double the number of stores the chain had by 1995, bringing our total to 1,000, and our strategy involved increasing the number of restaurants we had in towns and cities where we already had a sizeable presence, as well as expanding our outlets into hospitals and universities. We also struck a deal with Esso to place satellite stores in their service stations. These locations would be owned by an established franchisee, and they would obtain their products and supplies from the full-service restaurant. The advantages were twofold: construction costs were much lower than for a full-sized store, making them very profitable; and since the owners were experienced, we also cut back dramatically on the training costs and time required to get the stores up and running. The strength of the Tim Hortons brand also generated additional business for Esso by attracting more customers.

In a kind of snowball effect, the increased franchise and consumer interest generated capital and cash flow that could be invested in rapid expansion. Though the target was 500 stores in five years, no one knew just how large the chain could become. The original plan was to open 200 stores a year, an objective we would eventually accomplish.

As the company grew, we also gained access to better real estate. During the late 1980s, we opened a number of stores on Highway 401 between Toronto and Montreal in locations operated by Scott's Hospitality. Not surprisingly, given the amount of traffic that passed by them every day, these stores did very well. Many of the outlets that were paired with a Wendy's restaurant did particularly strong business. This led me to consider whether Tim Hortons could develop a closer business relationship with Wendy's, a hamburger chain based in Ohio.

A partnership with Wendy's would allow us to acquire some real estate that was too expensive for a stand-alone Tim Hortons, and it was clear that the two chains did not compete for the same market. Tim Hortons was busiest in the early-morning periods, while Wendy's main business occurred at midday.

Hal Gould was president of Wendy's Canada and an acquaintance, so I inquired about the possibility of an arrangement between the two companies. It was then that he invited me to speak to Dave Thomas.

Dave was a legendary figure in the food-service industry, having entered the restaurant business as a teen. He eventually met Kentucky Fried Chicken founder Colonel Harland Sanders and, with Sanders' help, Dave turned four struggling Kentucky Fried Chicken restaurants into successes. He would later sell these first franchises, along with four more he had acquired, back to KFC and use the proceeds to open the first Wendy's in Columbus, Ohio, in 1969.

I had taken up golf when I turned sixty, and I'd heard Dave was a big fan of the sport, so I flew down to Florida to meet him for a game at the Adios Golf Club, an exclusive men's club in Coconut Creek. My aim was quite clear: TDL was interested in acquiring the rights to Wendy's in Canada. Since Thomas was the face of the business, it made sense to approach him first. He turned out to be a very likeable guy, very charismatic, with a quick sense of humour. Dave was a great salesman, and it showed in his personality. Though he had not been particularly active in the daily operations of Wendy's since the middle of the 1980s and was functioning more as the company's spokesman and face of its marketing efforts, Thomas agreed to arrange a meeting with the senior Wendy's executives to discuss my interest in the business.

Following our Florida golf game, several of Wendy's top executives, including chairman Jim Near and president Gord Teter, met with TDL at our offices in Oakville to discuss the possibility of acquiring the franchise rights to the burger chain in Canada. My vision, of course, was to develop stores with both brands under one roof, thereby growing both systems. However, we had no idea how diverse Wendy's master franchise agreement was or just how many problems faced the Canadian division of the company. Thomas had grown the business extremely quickly, and the company had opened 2,000 restaurants within its first decade and added another 1,000 by 1985. In order to generate that kind of growth, Wendy's had struck some unusual licensing arrangements with a variety of individuals, including selling master licences to a variety of jurisdictions in the world. We were unaware of many of these details when we originally approached Wendy's and were surprised to hear that the Canadian operation had significant financial problems and they were carrying a $50 million loss to that point.

"We're pleased that you are interested, Ron, but we don't really have a business to sell you," Teter told me. "But we like the idea of trying to work together."

Once I realized they had nothing to sell, I suggested a joint real-estate venture in which both chain's stores would occupy one location. Teter agreed. The real-estate development company would buy prime locations and build "combo stores" that would have Wendy's, Tim Hortons, and occasionally other restaurants under one roof. The concept appealed to everyone at the meeting and a deal was quickly struck to start a business called TimWen. Within a year, we would open the first stores under the new partnership.

Oddly enough, the first combo operation was not one planned by the new partnership. Danny Murphy, who owned several stores in Prince Edward Island, had heard of the new venture and wanted to open a combo unit in Montague, on the island's eastern end. The town had a small population, and both Wendy's and TDL were very reluctant to consider his proposition. Danny persisted, and with his agreement to assume all the costs, we agreed to let him go forward. We gave him all of the architectural and engineering designs and details for the unit, as well as marketing plans. Danny's confidence was well placed: the unit opened successfully and, much to our surprise, stayed viable. Danny would later take credit for the combo concept and for introducing me to Dave Thomas and Jim Near. I found this amusing because all the planning, design and investment with Wendy's were done by the design departments of both companies. In fact, Dave, Jim and I had a great game of gin rummy on the flight from Hamilton to Charlottetown. Their cards were cold and mine were very hot. This probably didn't enamour me much to them, but it was a very pleasant flight for me financially.

The P.E.I. store was not entirely representative of our plans; a new store in Beamsville, Ontario, was the first to be planned and developed by the new partnership. It was the 600th Tim Hortons in Canada. The feeling among the partners was that the new units could include other restaurants that didn't conflict with either Tim Hortons or Wendy's. In the case of the Beamsville operation, the building also included a Dairy Queen and a KFC. Not surprisingly, Tim Hortons was the largest revenue generator of the four. A second store in Burlington, at Mainway and Walker's Line, opened soon afterward.

The idea of the new outlets in Canada was that Tim Hortons owners would acquire the Wendy's franchises and operate both; this allowed the owners to lower their operating costs by sharing real estate charges and the expense of the building. Generally, the new stores were highly successful and allowed us to access major markets, and spots on major highways, across the country that we could not previously afford. However, as Tim Hortons continued to push forward with its lunch menu, our stores became more directly competitive with Wendy's.

My friendship with Dave Thomas continued as the partnership with Wendy's evolved. Since I had a home in Florida, we would regularly play golf at Adios, where I became a member. Thomas's career, in many ways, had mirrored mine. He was not well educated but he had an entrepreneur's touch and had developed what appeared to be a remarkably successful franchise system. He was charming, something that came across in the hundreds of television advertisements he did for Wendy's, and also very competitive.

ooooo

As the trial with Lori Horton continued throughout the early 1990s, I began reflecting on how TDL should be operated in the long term. I was nearing the age of sixty-five, and had been operating the company for nearly thirty years. I had always viewed myself as an employee of TDL who worked for the franchise owners; it was important to me that the company have some stability and be able to effectively deal with the issue of succession. I was concerned for the future of the business should something happen to me. I also worried the impact such an occurrence might have on the stores.

Although I never had conceived of Tim Hortons as a family business, all of my seven children had worked for the company in some capacity. My daughter, Rhonda, and my son Steven both worked for the Tim Horton Children's Camps, while the others, Ron Jr., Gary, Darrel and Derrick, either owned stores or worked for TDL. But none of them had displayed the abilities or interest in running TDL. However, my son Grant, who had studied business at the University of Western Ontario and later moved to Asia to study languages, appeared to demonstrate the skills needed to manage the expansive business that Tim Hortons had become. During his time in Asia, he worked for the Sumitomo Mitsui Bank, one of Japan's largest financial institutions, and his ability to speak several languages fluently made him a desirable business asset. I began wondering whether Grant might have the ability to take over the reins at TDL. I called him and asked him to return to Canada and join the management team.

"Dad, I'll come back and join the company on the basis that I move to the province of Quebec," he said, adding that he wanted to improve his ability to speak French. He was given a position in public relations as a means of learning the business, but I was never convinced that he was truly interested in taking over TDL, or at least he never indicated a compelling desire to do so. Still, he did well in his initial positions with TDL, and I began moving him up the executive ladder in Quebec.

Throughout his time at TDL, Grant had a great mentor in executive vice-president Arch Jollymore. But after personal matters altered Arch's role at TDL, Grant did not have the same support structure. In 1993 Paul House was appointed to the role of executive vice-president, and he effectively ran daily operations. Paul was given a free hand to manage my company—which, of course, is what you do if you are trying to groom a senior executive to take charge. However, one of the ramifications is that under Paul and without Arch's support, Grant failed to make progress within the business. Since it was becoming increasingly unlikely that Grant would succeed me in running TDL, I started considering other options.

One of the possibilities was to take TDL public. At the time, though it was clear that this option would create a financial windfall, the thought of it gave me pause. Certainly all of the major investment brokers were enthusiastic about the interest TDL would receive should it end up on the Toronto Stock Exchange. Some had suggested an offering could value the company at up to 20 times earnings, which in 1993 was around $18 million. That pegged the value of the business at between $360 million and $400 million, a far cry from the $10,000 I invested in 1966.

However, I was reluctant to pursue the idea of a public offering. I had little interest in the road shows needed to sell investors on the company, or all the time that would have to be spent briefing analysts on the business. It seemed like an intimidating arena to enter. Years later, after I had spent time on the boards of public companies, it became clear to me that my fears had been unfounded. The process of road shows and annual meetings seem to be more rehearsed and presented in a controlled environment. But at the time, I was unconvinced that a public offering was the right path for TDL.

For years, I attended a food-service conference in the U.S. held by Philip Morris, the parent company of Kraft General Foods. During the conference, held at the PGA National Golf Resort in 1994, Bernie

Syron, the chair of Cara Foods, and I decided to have dinner together to discuss the possibility of merging the companies. Since Cara was a publicly traded company, under his proposal TDL would go public and would be the largest shareholder of the new entity. It was a way of taking TDL to the public markets without the trial of a public offering. The concept had some merit, and I agreed it should be discussed further following our return to Canada.

We met again in Toronto a few weeks later and quietly began investigating the possibility of whether a deal could be struck. Though I'd initially approached the idea with a degree of hesitancy, as the concept unfolded I grew enthusiastic about its chances of succeeding. The deal would still have to have been sold to the Phelan family, who controlled Cara, and it was not clear they would have supported the idea. It did get to the board of directors, but a significant hurdle became apparent in the combo stores co-owned by Tim Hortons and Wendy's. Cara owned Harvey's, the Canadian hamburger chain, so there was a potential conflict of interest. Of course, this could have been resolved by spinning off the combo stores or by converting the Harvey's brand to Wendy's, which at that time was struggling. There was also a possibility for synergy: Harvey's had a significant number of stores in Quebec, where Wendy's had very few. But the deal took a different direction once Gord Teter at Wendy's was approached about the potential of a conflict. Once he became aware that Tim Hortons was open to a sale or a merger, Gord's interest was piqued.

"I had no idea you were looking to sell the company," he told me. "We'd love to have Tim Hortons. Let's talk about this."

Within days, the conversation with Teter would lead to the biggest transformation TDL and Tim Hortons had undergone since I acquired the Horton stake nearly three decades earlier.

15

WENDY'S WORLD

On August 8, 1995, Wendy's made a public announcement that it would acquire TDL and the Tim Hortons brand. The sale of the quintessential Canadian business generated huge headlines in Canadian newspapers, with the media valuing the deal at around $600 million.

While Cara Foods remained interested in some sort of merger with TDL right up until the acquisition by Wendy's was announced, we had to determine what would be the best arrangement for Tim Hortons and its owners. One of the considerations was where the future of Tim Hortons rested. If the business was to become a success in the United States, then it seemed to make sense to pursue a deal with Wendy's as opposed to going any further with Cara, which had a limited presence south of the border. Though few in the media were aware of how the sale to Wendy's had come about, the management team at TDL worked frantically for weeks, leading up to my meeting with Wendy's senior management in Ancaster at the start of August.

The deal was a complex transaction that was structured as a pooling of assets. In order to facilitate the arrangement, an Ontario company was formed called TimWen, and I received shares that could be exchangeable into common shares of Wendy's International Inc. on a one-for-one basis. The benefit to structuring the transaction in this fashion was that I would only pay tax on the shares when I exchanged them for Wendy's common shares. However, the deal was also structured so that I would have to exchange all of my TimWen shares for Wendy's common shares by no later than 2006, the date that would mark the tenth anniversary of the sale of TDL. Of course, this was a very attractive arrangement, even more so than was commonly reported by the press. The true value of the transaction has never been written about accurately.

I was certainly convinced that the deal was fair and represented the real value of the company. Though other offers might have resulted in a higher cash payment, I was encouraged by my advisers to take Wendy's stock with the expectation that it would appreciate by six or seven dollars per share with the announcement of the deal.

By making it a stock-based transaction, the upside was that Tim Hortons' expansion would go forward uninterrupted. As part of the sale, I was also given a five-year contract, the title of senior chairman and a salary of approximately $850,000 (Canadian) per year—Dave Thomas was receiving U.S.$850,000 as senior chairman of Wendy's—to be a part of the TDL business strategy. The deal allowed me to spend as much or as little time working at TDL as I wanted. I was also given 150,000 options per year, and a guarantee of two seats on the board of directors, which I felt would allow me to have some degree of influence over Wendy's business and strategy.

One of the keys to the deal was making sure that Wendy's would leave the management and system we had developed at TDL in place.

"Don't mess with the management," I told Gord Teter and Jim Near during our negotiations. "We have a great system in place and this is a great business." Both men agreed with me. To this day, Wendy's management has largely left untouched the team I put in place at TDL. It would not have been hard for them to make the mistake of changing the executive structure at TDL given that, in the months after the sale, there were a number of Wendy's executives who were openly pursuing roles with TDL. To the credit of Near and Teter, they understood that they had acquired a great company with a great track record and an outstanding concept. When I stepped down as senior chairman in 2001, there were more than 2,050 Tim Hortons stores, of which 61 were combos. This success reinforces my belief in the concept.

Though the transaction was large and its details were numerous, it was determined that TDL would not employ an investment bank to work through and support us during the negotiations. Instead, we relied on our advisers and good-faith bargaining, and we also utilized the Toronto-based Torys law firm as our legal advisers. While it was clear Wendy's had thoroughly examined the business plan and supporting data of TDL, no one on our side, including me, once raised the possibility that Wendy's future might not have been as bright as it initially appeared. There was never a suggestion that Wendy's might not be the best fit for Tim Hortons.

From the week when the preliminary terms of the sale were worked out at the gala in Burlington at the start of August, to the announcement of the deal, we worked frantically behind the scenes to try to assuage the owners' apprehensions about the impact of what we viewed as a "merger." In order to meet with as many people as possible, TDL set up a road show to detail the transaction to all of the Tim Hortons store owners across Canada. There was a pressing need to make our franchisees aware as soon as possible because, as a publicly traded company, Wendy's was concerned about word of the deal hitting the financial markets before it was officially announced. With that in mind, we organized eight regional meetings—Vancouver, Calgary, Winnipeg, northern Ontario, Quebec, southern Ontario, Nova Scotia and Newfoundland. For three days we toured the country, using the company's aircraft to get out and inform all of the owners as to what was taking place.

At these meetings, I addressed the owners, and then Teter spoke for Wendy's. We did our best to detail what changes they could expect to result from the sale. I reassured them and made them aware that I would be remaining on in a management role. Immediately following our presentations, we took questions from the owners. They expressed surprise at the deal and asked many questions. One of the facets they were most concerned about was whether there would be cross-selling of products between the two chains. In other words, would Wendy's be selling Tim Hortons coffee? Once they were assured that this wouldn't be the case and the two companies would remain separate, they seemed generally supportive of the deal.

It took another four months, until January 1, 1996, for the transaction to be finalized. In the meantime, TDL eclipsed its goal of opening 1,000 stores by the end of 1995, and actually managed to open an additional 262 new outlets that year alone for a total of 1,262. By the start of 1996, with thousands of eager prospective franchise owners and the added interest of existing owners looking to open new stores, it was easy to open new restaurants. It appeared likely that the chain would double in size again within five years, which was the game plan—as summarized by the theme of "2,000 stores by 2000"—which had been our mission long before the sale was completed.

While Tim Hortons' performance continued to exceed all expectations, my deal with Wendy's was problematic almost from the start. By the end of the first quarter of 1996—less than three months after the sale was closed—problems arose with dividend payments on the shares I owned. The dividends amounted to roughly U.S.$4 million annually and would only be taxable in Canada. It seemed like a clear enough arrangement, and had been approved by lawyers on both sides of the sale prior to the deal's closing.

In March, I heard a rumour that Wendy's would withhold tax on the annual dividends, at a rate of 15 percent or approximately U.S.$600,000. This, of course, also meant I would be paying tax twice. I contacted the chief financial officer about it, and he admitted that Wendy's had been advised to withhold the money. Even after I offered a personal guarantee that I would hold them harmless should a tax ruling go against Wendy's, the company would not relent. Wendy's agreed that this move ran contrary to the terms of the sale of Tim Hortons, but they still decided to withhold the money.

I went to our tax adviser, Laurie Pare at Price Waterhouse in Calgary, to see what could be done about the issue. He came to the conclusion that it was double taxation and did not comply under the U.S.–Canada tax rules; he appealed the issue, successfully, to the U.S. Internal Revenue Service. After receiving the rulings from the tax department, I contacted Wendy's vice-president of finance, Ron Musick, and Gord Teter. I indicated that I wanted the situation to be dealt with, and that I was prepared to launch a lawsuit against Wendy's if the situation was not resolved. Teter was clearly concerned about the optics of the situation, and his management team came to Oakville, where we negotiated a settlement that involved Wendy's paying interest at more than 20 percent on the withheld money, retroactive to the start of the dispute. It was a very expensive deal for

Wendy's. The tax agreement continued throughout the entire period of time that I was with the company, and as long as I held Wendy's shares. As far I know, this agreement was never disclosed to the board or written in the proxy statements, and to me this showed some of the underlying weakness of their management.

Unfortunately, the battle over the withheld funds created a significant rift between me and several of the executives at Wendy's. They remained courteous to me personally, but blocked every move I tried to put forward with the company from that point onward. My suggestions for operational improvements, based on my experience at TDL, were never taken seriously.

The tax issue may not appear significant to some, but in retrospect it was a sign of things to come in my dealings with Wendy's. It did not take long for it to become clear that their top executives, including Gord Teter and Dave Thomas, thought they had come out ahead in the TDL transaction and were not going to allow me input into the operations of our combined company. Though I was Wendy's largest shareholder, I was relegated to the sidelines as far as the business went. Some may be surprised to learn that Dave was not always the avuncular personality that he projected in the television commercials. Certainly he was a very charismatic figure, but he also understood Wendy's corporate culture and how to operate in the background. And despite owning only a fraction of the shares I held, Thomas had control over the board, many of whom had been appointed by him personally. The board members largely deferred to Dave, even though he had long since stepped away from managing the company's daily operations.

My feelings of alienation worsened following the death of Wendy's chairman Jim Near in July 1996. Near was someone I had grown to trust over the months I had known him, and I felt like I had lost a great deal when he died. My discomfort grew throughout the second half of the 1990s, as it became clear that the management of Wendy's, under Teter, was not performing up to the expectations of shareholders. Rather than get the expected boost after the Tim Hortons deal, Wendy's stock actually dropped. By July 1996, it was trading as low as U.S.$16.75.

It also turned out that Wendy's was buying back franchises and reselling them, recording the revenue as profit. This gambit, which included sizeable margins on real estate, was not disclosed to the investment community. In 1998, financial analysts caught on to the method Wendy's was using to increase its profits, and forced the company to clarify its revenue and earnings figures. Meanwhile, as Wendy's struggled to expand its hamburger-restaurant business and improve its bottom line, Tim Hortons continued to grow after the acquisition and generated huge cash flow for the parent company. It was clear that Tim Hortons was outperforming the much larger Wendy's. Tim Hortons was the jewel in the crown.

My issues with Wendy's corporate governance became even more pronounced after the sudden death of Gord Teter, who was serving as both CEO and chairman of the company. Teter's passing, just before Christmas 1999 after a bad bout of the flu, left a hole in Wendy's already questionable executive structure. Dave Thomas immediately stepped in to fill the void through his role as executive chairman. Then, a special management committee, consisting of Thomas, Frederick Reed and chief operating officer Jack Schuessler, along with Paul House and me, was put in charge of overseeing the company's operations.

Another long-time director, James Pickett, joined me on a selection committee designed to find a replacement for Teter. The process took several months, but eventually we found two candidates who were clearly qualified to take over the chief executive role. Despite our recommendations, Dave Thomas kept putting forth Schuessler as the right man for the position. That didn't sit well with me. I didn't think Schuessler had the strong personality or vision necessary to move Wendy's forward.

On a Saturday early in March, I received a call from Pickett about the CEO decision.

"Ron, Dave has decided that Jack Schuessler is going to take over as CEO," he told me.

I was shocked by the news, especially since the board-approved selection committee had had nothing to do with the decision. Thomas's disproportionate influence over the board of directors meant that he could push them to approve Schuessler's appointment, even if he wasn't the best candidate for the job. I became determined to talk Schuessler out of taking the position, and asked him to come and meet with me at Jetport, my air-charter company at the Hamilton airport.

When he arrived, I tried to convince him it was not in his or the company's best interest to have him appointed as CEO. Wendy's needed someone with proven leadership skills and the business acumen to move the company ahead of competition like McDonald's and Burger King.

"Jack, you just aren't the right guy for the issues facing this company. Stay on as president and we'll bring in our candidate. In a couple of years we'll move him to chairman and you can take over as CEO."

"No, Ron, I want this job," he replied.

Since I was unable to talk Schuessler out of accepting the role, the board supported Thomas as expected, though I protested and voted against the appointment. The whole saga of finding a replacement for Teter demonstrated the power that Thomas had at Wendy's. The company's best interest was to find a new external candidate to replace Teter, one with the vision to assess a highly competitive market and determine what Wendy's should look like in the years ahead. But Thomas wanted Schuessler because he knew he would be his "yes" man. It was just another example of how weak the company's management was. The whole issue left me even more disenchanted with the way the company was running and my investment in it.

With Schuessler's appointment as CEO, my situation at Wendy's had clearly become untenable. I had no influence on the business side, and it was obvious that, under the current management team, Wendy's was being outperformed by its competition. I came to the realization that I had sold Tim Hortons, a great business success built on a solid foundation, to a company I believe was poorly managed and maintained. Though I remained the largest shareholder by a wide margin, I had no influence over the situation. There was no way I could enact changes in the operations at Wendy's. Yet I felt it was vital to protect my sizeable investment in the business. I knew the company's problems could be resolved if the strategy that built Tim Hortons was applied to Wendy's. But the only way that was going to happen was if I managed to work with the corporation, away from Thomas and his friends on the board of directors.

In retrospect, it was clear Wendy's had done a lot of due diligence on TDL and Tim Hortons and was aware that ours was a strong, rapidly growing business with tremendous cash flow. While they had investigated every angle on Tim Hortons, I had clearly not been as thorough in considering all the potential problems with Wendy's. Given the difficulty of the situation I had placed myself in, I spent the months following Schuessler's appointment as CEO looking for ways to extricate myself from the deal.

The one option that immediately came to mind was a takeover of Wendy's. That would have required me to buy more Wendy's shares, force out the directors who remained loyal to Dave, and bring in new directors and executives who were focused on fixing Wendy's many problems. Given the fact the company's stock price had not improved significantly since the Tim Hortons acquisition, it would have been an expensive but workable way of taking control of the business.

Unfortunately, the lawyers I employed to help plan the takeover informed me of a major roadblock: state law in Ohio, where Wendy's was based, made a hostile takeover nearly impossible.

Ohio's strange share acquisition law has been called "economic folly" by some economists. It strips away the voting rights of shares purchased through a hostile tender offer or large open-market transaction. In order to win back the voting rights, those parties attempting the hostile takeover must win a special shareholder vote held fifty days after the shares are acquired. Of course, directors who are about to lose their jobs rarely vote in support of a hostile takeover bid. Needless to say, few such gambits have been successful in Ohio in recent years. The law, variations of which are now in place in several U.S. states, was meant to keep corporate raiders from taking over a business and either breaking it up or moving jobs outside of the state. However, the law rarely functioned to protect jobs; rather, it was now used to protect badly run businesses from investors who felt they could improve operations and shareholder value.

Even with the legislation, Wendy's senior management was concerned about the possibility of a takeover and instituted a "shareholder rights" plan. More commonly known as a "poison pill," the plan was designed to ward off any investor who might be willing to take a run at Wendy's. This manoeuvre made it clear that this wasn't a company with a lot of confidence in its management or governance, but instead was fearful of outside interests attempting to acquire the business.

While one law firm—Milbank, Tweed, Hadley & McCloy— suggested that we might make a successful play for Wendy's despite the Ohio law, Jere Thomson, the New York securities lawyer with Jones Day whom we retained, made it clear that a hostile takeover would be difficult and costly.

"If you are at all successful, you'll be looking at six or seven years and it will cost millions," he told me. "They will do anything to discredit you. It will be a dirty fight."

The only hope of taking over Wendy's, according to Thompson, was to gain some support from the board of directors and launch a proxy fight, a method of convincing shareholders to force the board to bring in new management. But I had no support on the board. It had become apparent I would not be able to influence Wendy's or protect my investment in the business.

Despite my inability to go forward with a takeover bid, we learned that Wendy's senior management had become aware that I'd been considering the option. Needless to say, Wendy's executives, who had not been friendly to me for some time, grew even more reluc-tant to address my concerns about the company. I was pushed to the outside and rarely consulted on any matter relating to the company's strategy.

In the meantime, Tim Hortons continued to surpass expectations, moving forward with the expansion plan devised a decade earlier. Due to the increasing success of TDL, I wasn't the only one interested in acquiring Wendy's during the period. Soon after I determined that a takeover bid would prove to be too difficult and costly to mount, I received a call from Gary Bettman, the commissioner of the National

Hockey League. Bettman knew me from my ownership of the Flames, and he asked me for a few minutes of my time.

"Ron, I've got a friend named Nelson Peltz and he asked me to give you a call," Bettman explained. "He knows you are the largest shareholder of Wendy's and wants to sit down and have a talk with you about the business."

Though I had not met Peltz, I was aware of his reputation as a corporate raider. Peltz was the head of a company called Triarc, but he had a long history in business. In his younger days, he made his reputation by taking his family's food business and growing it into a $150 million publicly traded company by 1978. Along the way, he started a small investment fund that grew by putting money into solid businesses that had fallen on hard times and resurrecting those companies. His greatest win came in 1997, when he acquired the iced-tea maker Snapple for just U.S.$300 million and sold it thirty months later for U.S.$1.45 billion, giving him a 383 percent gain on his investment. He also had an interest in the food-service business, through his ownership of the Arby's chain.

I agreed to meet with Peltz, and he flew in his Boeing 727 to the Hamilton airport to speak to me. He explained that he was hoping to mount a takeover of Wendy's. Having investigated the possibility of such a bid, I told Peltz it would be a difficult and expensive undertaking.

"Well, Ron, at the very least, can you see if you can arrange a meeting with Dave Thomas?" he asked.

I called Dave at his home in Florida. I felt that if Peltz could increase shareholder value, the very least Wendy's management could do was to speak to him.

"Look, Dave, Nelson Peltz came to meet with me and hoped I could set up a meeting for him with you," I explained. "I don't know much about the gentleman, but it seems like he has some interesting thoughts on improving shareholder value." He agreed, and said he would like to meet with him.

It wasn't long after I called Dave that Schuessler called me in Hamilton.

"There's no way we are going to talk to Nelson Peltz, and we're pretty disappointed you even met with him," Schuessler told me.

It was indicative of the approach used by Schuessler. The company hoped it could bury its head in the sand and its problems would go away.

Out of options, I determined that my best course of action was to disassociate myself from Wendy's, which meant selling my 16.8 million shares. At the time, Wendy's stock was resting around $25, and the Canadian dollar was trading at 63 cents U.S. The weakness of the Canadian dollar would compensate for the fact that the shares had not appreciated significantly (in U.S. funds) in the five years I held them.

But by this time, Wendy's was very anxious to have me removed from the board of the company. Dave Thomas was sick with liver cancer, and it was clear that the senior executives at Wendy's, including Jack Schuessler, were very concerned about the role I might assume, given my position as the company's largest shareholder. Thomas had actively blocked the moves I had tried to make at Wendy's, but with him out of the picture, there were worries within the executive suite about what I might do. With that in mind, Wendy's made an offer to buy back shares totalling $250 million at the current market price, and I gave up my seat on the board since I had stopped attending the directors' meetings.

As the negotiations to sell the majority of my stock progressed into October 2001, I was invited to go fishing with former U.S. President

George H.W. Bush at Hilton Head Island, and then spend some time in Florida. I had been introduced to the president by Peter Pocklington, the former owner of the Edmonton Oilers, and had been on one previous fishing trip with him at Tree River, north of the Arctic Circle. After our fishing tournament in Hilton Head ended, the president, Peter and I flew to Marathon, Florida. In one of the great thrills of my life, I rode in the back of the car with former President Bush for the forty-mile drive to the Cheeka Lodge in Islamorada. For the duration of our trip, the car was accompanied by four state police motorcycles, several marked cruisers and several unmarked cars. It was a remarkable level of security for a couple of guys who were going fishing.

The deal with Wendy's became finalized soon after we arrived in Florida, and the company flew its in-house counsel down to have me sign the final paperwork. Once that was done, he handed me a cheque for U.S.$250 million.* This would give some indication of the urgency to finalize the deal.

For the company's controller, it was business as usual. He couldn't have understood the significance of the cheque he was handing me, which officially ended my tenure with TDL and Tim Hortons, the company I had nurtured, after thirty-seven years.

---

* As part of the sale of TDL, I had a ten-year period from the signing of the deal in January 1996 in which to sell my shares. In the end, the 5.8 million shares I owned after the October 2001 deal with Wendy's were sold in 2002.

16

AFTER TIMS

Though it has only been a few years since I severed my ties with Wendy's completely, it has already become apparent that there is no easy way to defend the deal to sell TDL to the burger chain. In retrospect, the sale, which I viewed as a merger at the time, was not as well structured as it should have been and we should have conducted a more thorough review of Wendy's operations.

However, while TDL can shoulder some of the blame for not comprehending Wendy's operational issues, I would maintain that the real reason the arrangement failed to stand the test of time remains Wendy's inability to contribute measurably to the merger. While Tim Hortons' dramatic expansion continued after the sale, Wendy's stalled. While Tim Hortons has doubled its stores in the past ten years, Wendy's has struggled to open new stores, and many of those it has opened are owned by the company and bloated with additional costs. If Wendy's had brought anything close to the level of cash flow that

Tim Hortons brought to the deal, the company's stock would have appreciated dramatically over the years I was the largest single shareholder. But Wendy's simply did not perform, leaving Tim Hortons as the company's only means of growth.

By the beginning of 2005, Tim Hortons' income outpaced that of Wendy's, though the chain had only a third of the stores and did not generate as much revenue. The number of Tim Hortons stores grew from 1,033 to 2,694 stores in the ten-year period starting in 1994, while Wendy's, which had 4,411 stores in 1994, grew to 6,745 stores. On top of that, many of Wendy's company-owned stores, which accounted for 22 percent of its overall number, which in my opinion was an unusually high number for a franchise system, began to struggle with costs, creating a drag on the chain's profitability. The operating margin of TDL has been around 25 percent, while Wendy's has been lucky to make single-digit margins. Tim Hortons restaurants averaged $1.7 million in sales in 2004, and revenue growth for the chain over the last decade was 406 percent. The chain made a profit of $191 million in 2005 and now controls an estimated 76 percent of the Canadian coffee and baked-goods sector. On the other hand, revenue growth at Wendy's during the same period was only 50 percent and the chain has been forced to close many underperforming stores.*

Wendy's had international divisions in many parts of the world, and they were all losing money—Britain, Greece, Japan, Argentina, New Zealand, Mexico, the Caribbean islands and many others. The

---

* Many accomplishments of the TDL system could easily be shown if a graph was created to demonstrate the company's revenue and store growth from inception until now. This graph would show an upward trend for every year the company has been in operation, with the single exception of 1991, the year the GST was introduced. In that year, growth was flat across TDL and almost every food services business. I am proud of the many men, women and families who have significantly improved their financial well-being by owning a Tim Hortons franchise over the past 40 years.

company's writedowns of these losses were staggering. Under Dave Thomas and his management team, Wendy's was not selective about granting master licences in foreign markets. There was virtually no support because they didn't have the support staff in place to monitor stores in faraway countries. It didn't take long for Wendy's to start closing many of these operations.

Without a doubt, my sale of Tim Hortons to Wendy's was a bad deal. But at the time all signs pointed to the fact that we seemed to be getting a fair price.

A decade after the sale of TDL, the Tim Hortons chain has been valued by some at more than $4 billion, a figure that makes it more valuable than Wendy's, which has more than twice the number of restaurants.

I was certainly interested when, in 2005, I first heard that hedge funds—large, privately held investment vehicles—were sizing Wendy's up as a possible takeover target. Many of these funds acquire large stakes in distressed companies, set their financial houses straight, and then sell them at a significant profit. With vast reserves of capital behind them, their demands are harder to ignore than those of a single shareholder such as myself. One of the obvious ways of improving Wendy's outlook was to spin off Tim Hortons via an initial public offering (IPO). Such a sale would raise a large amount of cash. Among those urging Wendy's to consider a Tim Hortons IPO was U.S.–based Pershing Square Capital Management, which had acquired a large block of Wendy's stock. Pershing was led by William Ackman, and soon after his firm started acquiring shares, I called and spoke with him about the direction his investment would take. He was interested in speaking with me further, and flew to Toronto for a meeting.

By this time, the problems with Wendy's management were regularly being brought up in the press. The situation seemed to settle for several months, as the hedge funds worked in the background in an attempt to do what I hadn't been prepared to undertake in 1994: take Tim Hortons onto the stock market through an IPO. Eventually Wendy's acquiesced, agreeing to spin off 18 percent of Tim Hortons in the spring of 2006. That would not be the end of the story, though.

Other interested investors approached me during this time, sounding out my thoughts on a takeover. Some even wanted me to participate, but I declined. However, a couple of funds did seek me out in the hope I would become an investor in a possible takeover, and I was amenable to that sort of investment.

Against this background, it was not altogether surprising to see Nelson Peltz, who had spoken to me privately about a takeover of Wendy's four years earlier, publicly announce he had taken a large stake in Wendy's in December 2005. Peltz had acquired 5.5 percent of the company and he began pushing the chain to spin off all of Tim Hortons, a move that would be particularly lucrative for the hedge funds. Initially, Wendy's balked at Peltz's power play, but in time, Jack Schuessler recognized that he wouldn't be able to keep the hedge funds at bay. They had simply acquired too many shares. The first part would be offered in an IPO, with the remainder being given to Wendy's shareholders. As if to demonstrate that Peltz had won, Schuessler even agreed to give him three seats on the Wendy's board. It is interesting to note that Nelson Peltz managed to force Wendy's to sell off Tim Hortons and put three of his nominees on the board. Strangely enough, Jack Schuessler resigned. But the challenges were really started by Bill Ackman, who managed to accumulate more than 10 percent of the shares.

The IPO was a great coup for the hedge funds. But if one looks at where Wendy's value and competitive position ended up under the Schuessler regime, the question has to be asked: Where will this mess end?

The IPO went forward at the end of March, and proved to be one of the most exciting events the Toronto Stock Exchange had seen in some time. Shares soared 23 percent the first day they were available, and the public was particularly keen on getting even a small ownership stake in the restaurant where they purchased their morning coffee.

Of course, the IPO was forced on Wendy's—Peltz had pressured the company to make a decision they didn't want to make. Was it a good thing? The senior management at Wendy's was well rewarded for the decision, especially if they held stock. And management at Tim Hortons was also rewarded. It was a great deal. The IPO raised $783 million, which translates into a total value on the company of around $5 billion. However, after the IPO, Tim Hortons shares have struggled to maintain their momentum. Only time will tell how they perform once the hype and interest has subsided.

Not surprisingly, as co-founder of the company I was not given any opportunity to buy Tim Hortons shares at the issuing price. Many people called and asked if I was buying shares in the aftermarket. In several business publications I was quoted saying that I would not be buying Tim Horton shares. It never ceases to amaze me that the press chooses the negative side of my comments. What I in fact said was that the shares would be fully valued on the opening day and I would not be buying into the issue at that price, seeing as there was a great deal of hype about the stock. The stock traded in huge numbers and reached $37.99, much higher than its issue price of $27.00. At the time of this writing, the price has dropped below the issue price. My belief was when the IPO came out, Wendy's stock, in the low $40s, was the real opportunity. The stock climbed to over $66 and it is still trading around $60.

I believe the Tim Horton brand is a very solid business that has long-term growth potential, but this will depend on decisions made in the best interests of the store owners first, and it is in the best interests of everyone to make this happen. The food service industry changes often and always will, which is no different than all businesses, really. The food industry is one of the largest in the world for obvious reasons and only those who can adapt to change will prosper and grow.

One of the great truisms of life is that people will go out of their way to have a good experience. Dining out is a form of entertainment and people will return over and over again to enjoy the product served by well-managed restaurants that serve good food, whether it's steak, lobster or something as simple as coffee and a donut or bagel. Tim Hortons is a business that was built on that premise.

∞∞∞∞

Given my historical role with the company, many people have approached me with questions about the future of Tim Hortons. Clearly, there are still areas in which the company has the potential to grow, though it is more difficult in some parts of Canada—for example, in Atlantic Canada, where penetration is heavy—than in others. The kiosk concept that has proven so effective over the past fifteen years still works well for the company and its franchisees and the company may build out more by developing these further.

In Canada, there is currently no major competition for Tim Hortons. Beginning in 2001, when U.S.–based Krispy Kreme opened its first location in Mississauga, Ontario, it appeared that the chain might make some serious inroads into the Canadian donut business, but I was never as bullish as many other observers were. I had been to many Krispy Kreme outlets in the United States prior to the chain's arrival in Canada, and never thought of it as a viable enterprise. It was far too focused on one product, and after all, how many donuts can you eat? I wonder if the basis of Krispy Kreme's business was faulty. Krispy Kreme relies on its donuts being served hot, a concept promoted by lighting up a sign that told customers the donuts were hot. But how many times a day can that sign really be lit up? And what happens when it isn't? Customers learn to stay away.

On the coffee side of the business, Starbucks has emerged, but the business's higher pricing limits its audience. Discriminating coffee drinkers, who like stronger coffee, are clearly in the minority in Canada, which is why Starbucks has never truly been a rival for Canadians' affection. Tim Hortons simply continues to dominate the market.

Canadians continue to be drawn to Tim Hortons coffee, to the point that the company has become part of the country's social fabric. In many ways, current Canadians have grown up around Tim Hortons and accepted the company's coffee almost as the standard. And they come back again and again because the coffee is always fresh and the restaurants are clean and inviting. It is these basics that most of our competitors could never match.

The question at the moment is whether the culture of Tim Hortons can remain the same within a publicly traded structure. Since my departure in January 2001, senior management at Tim Hortons has begun altering its relationship with franchise owners by placing pressure on their margins. When I owned the company, the number one customer of TDL was the restaurant owner. They were the backbone of the company; they were what made the system work. They are on the front lines, dealing face to face with the customer, and are therefore integral to the company's success. Any change to that could have dramatic ramifications for the company in the long run.

Obviously, many are looking for Tim Hortons to expand further into the U.S. Many of those stores have struggled to be profitable, but that follows the company's typical expansion pattern. We also had a tough time making things work in Quebec and western Canada, but eventually turned those locations into high-volume stores. The same was true of our stores in Buffalo, but those stores also do very well now. If the formula that made Tim Hortons work so well in Canada isn't changed, the chain should eventually break into the U.S. market in a significant way. There isn't that much of a difference between Americans and Canadians when it comes to what they eat. If the quality is there, as it is in Canada, Americans will go to Tim Hortons. Some feel Tim Hortons could add another 1,500 outlets in Canada, and to me that doesn't seem an unreasonable goal.

Clearly, Tim Hortons has faced some growing pains in recent times. Among these problems was the uproar that occurred when it became common knowledge that the company was using frozen food that was then defrosted and finished in the stores.

Though freshness has always been a hallmark for Tim Hortons, finding employees willing to produce products in the middle of the night, especially in the new stores in the United States, has long been a problem. In order to solve the dilemma, management determined that it would be prudent to begin using frozen baked goods, thus easing the franchisees' burden of producing fresh product from scratch.

It was a concept I had considered many years earlier. I approached a small chain in New Jersey called Donuts Galore, owned by Hersh Surkin, which had been producing its products then freezing them cryogenically. They were thawed at room temperature and served in their stores. In the end, the idea was dismissed because of concerns over the quality of the product and whether we could make it work across a chain as large as Tim Hortons. I was always concerned that shipping frozen product in large trucks was a losing proposition: it meant you were paying high fuel costs in order to transport a lot of bulk. To my way of thinking, it had always made more sense to ship the ingredients needed for baking donuts, muffins and cookies, than it did to ship frozen goods from one central Canadian location.

But with Tim Hortons' rapid expansion continuing as I was departing from the Wendy's board, the idea of using frozen product once again emerged. In 2001, the company announced a joint venture with Cuisine de France, a subsidiary of an Irish business, to develop a "par-bake" plant in Brantford, Ontario, a short drive west of Hamilton. When the deal was announced, few took notice—or asked what "par-bake" meant.

At the time, I felt it was wrong to keep the public in the dark about the move. Of course, in the early stages, for competitive reasons, it was necessary to keep the information about the initiative from circulating. But after many of the bugs in the system had been resolved, there was no reason not to make it public. Even after it leaked out and became one of the company's worst-kept secrets, TDL refused to acknowledge or explain the change.

In mid-October 2003, a reporter from the *Calgary Herald* called me asking about the frozen-product issue. I told the reporter that I was no longer part of the company's ownership and therefore was not the appropriate person to comment on TDL's business. I suggested she try to contact Bill Moir, the company's executive vice-president of marketing, who happened to be in Calgary for a regional meeting. After the reporter's call, I followed up with Moir and told him the media were picking up on the story. I asked him why TDL would not simply speak with the reporter and confirm the direction of the company.

He urged me not to speak to the press, and told me they weren't going to say anything about it and it would just go away. I told him that I wasn't going to pursue the matter, but that if I was asked about it further, I would be honest. The reporter called back the next day and said that Moir had not returned her call. I told her that I would be careful about my comments and acknowledged the new methods that were in place.

The story broke in the *Herald* on October 23, 2003, and confirmed what a large number of Tim Hortons' customers already knew. TDL management scrambled furiously to clarify the matter. For my part, the story in the Calgary paper only included half of my comments to the reporter, and much of the context of my quotes was lost in the article. I had told the reporter that the move to use frozen products would likely prove beneficial for Tim Hortons' operations in the future as they continued to work on improving quality. However, those remarks were left out of the story. To some store owners, it appeared that I had betrayed them, though that was far from the truth. I had tried to explain to the reporter the business reasons behind the move, but I believe the paper was more interested in sensationalizing the matter.

The fact that I went public on the matter after Moir refused to do so annoyed many store owners who felt I had leaked this questionable secret. I was told that some store owners even advocated a boycott of the Tim Horton Children's Camps, though it fortunately never came to that. Throughout it all, the management of TDL, most of whom I had hired personally, never defended me or took responsibility for their actions.

Truthfully, the idea of using frozen products thoroughly disappointed me. It wouldn't be done in Tim Hortons restaurants if I still owned the company, even if, in the long run, it may have been the best way to operate the chain. I probably would have modified the position so that the white and chocolate cake donuts—which are easily made with automated equipment and require minimal training to produce—continued to be freshly made. More than the change, however, the real failure was the company's communications strategy. They needed to convince the public that Tim Hortons' donuts and other baked goods would actually be more consistent; under the new system, they could be finished on demand, instead of in large batches only once or twice a day.

Instead of embracing the change and putting a positive spin on it, TDL was slow to admit they were using frozen product, and the store owners were sworn to secrecy. The plan was poorly conceived. There were simply too many people in the company to keep the move a secret. And rather than acknowledge the decision, TDL management chose to try to conceal it. The controversy reached its peak when the vice-president of communications told the media that "until I confirm or deny anything, it simply doesn't exist." That turned out to be a statement that made headlines across Canada. The sad part was that management had made the spokesperson hide the truth. Soon after this incident, that person no longer worked for the company.

Though they were upset with my decision to go public, the store owners were one of my main concerns when I heard the frozen food plan was being adopted. In my mind, franchisees have always been central to any new company initiative. I suspect that there was some degree of consultation with some of the store owners. But for those who didn't want to go forward with the plan, there was no alternative offered. TDL needed 100 percent of the owners to sign on. The frozen-product initiative turned out to be costly for some owners. An owner who had just opened a new store, for example, was faced with replacing all of their baking equipment with freezers and other equipment, with very little compensation.

I always felt that management handled this issue poorly. I think the decision to go forward with frozen product was made so far above the franchisee level that there was no regard for the store owners' opinions. The decision had been made, and that was the way it would be, regardless of any opposition.

It made me feel terrible when store owners and TDL management would blame me for making the news public. I would regularly be approached by franchisees at social functions who believed that I was the one who had called the press and made the story public, though I never called a reporter on the issue.

It was never clear to me why everyone in management was so ashamed of the frozen products. While they were initially of much lesser quality than what had been sold previously, they have improved greatly since then, though they will never be as good as the fresh product we prepared completely in the stores. And since stores no longer need to bake batches of donuts or muffins at once, the displays are no longer as appetizing. All of this has proven my earlier predictions correct. Increasingly, Tim Hortons has become a coffee business. Coffee and beverage sales are rapidly increasing and account for up to 70 percent of a store's revenue, while donuts, which once made up 80 percent of sales, now account for less than 10 percent.

ooooo

Though I have always enjoyed flying, there was never any plan to create a business out of it. But following the sale of Tim Hortons to Wendy's, I found myself in possession of two aircraft that had not been included in the deal. Since I was no longer flying as often as I had when I oversaw the expansion of Tim Hortons, I started an executive charter service. That led to the formation of Jetport, my charter service based in Hamilton.

Like most things in my life, it was never my intent to build my interest in flying into a company, but that's exactly what happened. Now Jetport is a vibrant, growing business with seven airplanes. It has great potential, especially as executives become increasingly disenchanted with all the difficulties of commercial flying in a post–September 11 world.

With Jetport up and running, I had no plans to launch any additional businesses. But as my difficulties with Wendy's increased, I began looking for an outlet to focus my energy on. Being goal-oriented, I felt the need to keep busy. Thus began Fox Harb'r Golf Resort and Spa.

In many ways, Fox Harb'r was part of my estate-planning process. After making sure my family was looked after, I decided to donate the balance of my estate to a charitable organization, which is still the case today. While working through the process, I began thinking about how the money from my estate would be spent. Obviously, I would have no control over this after my death, so I began to consider how I might give something back to my home province. It may sound sentimental or clichéd, but that's what I wanted to do. With this in mind, my focus fell on a piece of land I had acquired in Nova Scotia in 1987.

Georg Vogel, who had owned the land that became the Tatamagouche children's camp, approached me in July about considering another property nearby.

"Ron, there's an amazing piece of land in Fox Harbour," he explained. "I'd buy it, but I can't afford it. It is an incredibly picturesque setting, and once you see it, I know you'll want it."

After much discussion, he convinced me to at least go and look at the property. We took the half-hour drive to Fox Harbour and headed for the far western end of the property, which largely consisted of brush and swamp. Due to the overgrowth, we decided to walk along the shoreline that looked out at Prince Edward Island. It was a beautiful summer day, and after walking for a short time, we encountered an amazing rock formation. It was stunning, and as I looked at this majestic natural feature it was hard to believe that no one had purchased the property to that point.

From there, we crossed a small stream and proceeded up the other side to a point of land that cut out into the strait. Standing at that point, you could see most of the property's shoreline, which was more than three kilometres long.

As we were leaving the property, we saw a beat-up For Sale sign. Clearly the land had been on the market for some time, without any takers. I offered cash and a quick closure. We had arrived at the property at 10 a.m., and by 3 o'clock that afternoon, I owned it.

The only issue was that there were two or three smaller pieces of land in the middle of the parcel that were not included in the sale. These parts had been taken over by the provincial government because of non-payment of property taxes. Rather than see those smaller parts put up for a general tender, we acquired them by swapping some of the other land. It took about eighteen months for the entire transaction to be complete.

We now owned more than a thousand acres with approximately five miles of shoreline on a cape, but I didn't have any immediate plans for it. The land sat for a decade before I began considering what I would do with it. As the deal with Wendy's became more contentious, I began to focus on my land in Nova Scotia. In 1997, I began thinking about building a golf course on the site. I had become infatuated with the game ever since taking it up late in life, and though I am a terrible player, my journeys have allowed me access to some of the greatest courses in the world. I knew that if people were going to venture to this rural portion of Nova Scotia to play golf, my course would have to be spectacular. I wanted to build a facility that would rival some of the great clubs in Canada and around the world. One of the first decisions I made was to build a runway, making it feasible for private aircraft to fly directly to the site from all over North America and Europe.

Given the amount of overgrowth on the land, clearing it was an arduous process that took months. Once this task was complete, the runway and hangar were constructed.

The aim was to incorporate some of the coastline, which was breathtaking and afforded unobstructed views of the Northumberland Strait, into the golf course. In this way, we would follow in the tradition of the great links courses around the world. Canadian golf architect Graham Cooke was hired to design the course, which starts by weaving into the forest before emerging on links land near the sea. My goal was also to offer the best-conditioned golf course in the country.

The project continued to expand the more we pushed forward. Once the clubhouse was started, we began to deal with the need for accommodation. Since there were no high-quality hotels or inns nearby, we built suites on the property, with an eye towards providing a high degree of comfort for guests. We modelled these rooms after similar buildings I had seen at Cape Cod.

The entire project turned out to be a great economic benefit to the area, which wasn't far from where I grew up. The region still struggles to develop new employment, and the construction and operation of

Fox Harb'r has certainly helped stimulate the local economy. It now employs 150 people during golf season.

Though it is an exclusive facility, Fox Harb'r has hosted some of the world's greatest leaders, entertainers and businesspeople since it opened. *Golf Digest* said the course was the best new club in Canada in 2001, and Prince Edward, former U.S. President Bill Clinton, former British Prime Minister John Major and many leading businesspeople from around the world have visited.

ooooo

My other passion since my exit from Wendy's has been sailing. Purchasing a sailboat was something I first considered before the sale to Wendy's. My hope was to sail around the world, just as I had done in the navy, but in far greater style. I went as far as to actually make an offer on a large sailing yacht in the early 1990s, before I came to my senses and realized I still had a company to manage and would not be able to make appropriate use of such a sophisticated vessel.

The interest was rekindled in 2002, when I finally had enough free time. I have owned many powerboats, including a 63-foot Ferretti and a 73-foot Donzi sport fishing boat, but sailing was in my blood. I loved the quiet of the ocean that could only be experienced while sailing. I was specifically interested in purchasing a boat designed by Ed Dubois. It turned out that a boat was being built in New Zealand for sailing enthusiast Neville Creighton, but he had changed his mind, deciding that he wanted something faster. For my purposes, on the other hand, the boat was perfect. I wanted a fast sailboat that offered luxury and comfort. I wanted a boat that was capable of sailing in any body of water, and the cruising sloop, which was initially called *Harlequin,* was 41 metres long with a mast that was 54 metres high. It couldn't pass under any bridges in Eastern Canada, but it could go just about everywhere else.

I had planned to name the boat after Fox Harb'r and use it as a marketing tool for the golf course and resort. That necessitated a name change, so we chose the name *Destination Fox Harb'r*. The intent was not to take the boat around the world at once. Instead, after I took possession on December 31, 2002, I stayed in New Zealand to watch the America's Cup. Eventually I sailed on a tour of Fiji, Tonga, French Polynesia, including Bora Bora, and through to the Galapagos Islands. Along the way I invited friends to be guests on the boat and to spend a week or two as part of the tour. By the summer, I took the boat through the Panama Canal and up the Atlantic coast, with the objective of taking part in the annual race from Marblehead to Halifax.

That is where the problems began. The boat was registered in the Cayman Islands in order to allow easy access to destinations and ports around the world, and we had received advance assurances from Canadian customs that it would not be a problem to bring the boat into Canada for three months on a visitor's permit. However, before the race, a picture of *Destination Fox Harb'r* appeared in a Halifax newspaper. Soon afterwards we were told that if the boat was brought into Canada, it would be impounded for unpaid taxes.

This seemed like an extreme overreaction on the part of Canadian customs and ran contrary to what we had previously been told. After all, the boat was paid for with after-tax dollars and could not be built anywhere in Canada, so it had not taken work away from Canadian shipbuilders. In many ways, the boat was meant to promote Fox Harb'r and, in turn, to promote tourism to Nova Scotia. I have paid a lot of taxes in this country over my lifetime, and this seemed like an unfortunate way to be treated considering our initial good intentions.

It turned out that Canadian customs wanted duties that amounted to millions of dollars, or almost half the value of the entire boat. Eventually, cooler heads prevailed and they allowed it to enter the country for forty-eight hours. Since then, the boat has come back to Canada, taking guests out in the summer of 2004 as a public relations move for Fox Harb'r Golf Resort and Spa.

Despite the customs issues, *Destination Fox Harb'r* remains one of the great pleasures in my life and is the spot where I can often be found when the weather in Nova Scotia turns cold. It has truly become a unique ambassador for Canada, for Nova Scotia and for Fox Harb'r Resort and Spa.

17

YOUR FRIEND ALONG THE WAY

In 1999, I had the good fortune of being inducted into the Canadian Business Hall of Fame. The other inductees that evening were newspaper baron Conrad Black, who founded the *National Post* and owned dozens of other papers in Canada and the U.S., Jean Coutu, the pharmacist and entrepreneur who was CEO of the Jean Coutu Group, and the late Theodore Loblaw, founder of the Loblaws grocery chain.

The event, a black-tie gala, was held at the Metro Toronto Convention Centre on Front Street. I had never met Black, the effusive media magnate, so while we were backstage before being shown to the head table, I extended my hand to introduce myself. He walked past me without acknowledging my greeting, and it occurred to me that this was going to be a long evening. It threatened to be an awkward situation, considering that Conrad was seated next to me at the head table. But once we sat down, he turned to me and introduced himself.

"Tell me about this Tim Hortons business," he said, shaking my hand.

I related some of the history of the restaurant chain and some of its developments over the previous three decades and said I had merged with Wendy's three years earlier. I further explained that part of the deal made me the largest shareholder, with approximately 17 million shares. This information was already provided in the bio that had been given to those in attendance. Black asked about the value of the stock. You could sense he was doing the math in his head. Suddenly he broke into a broad smile.

"Well, hello my newest best friend!" he laughed. The rest of the dinner was tremendous fun, great conversation. For Black, businesses were measured in dollars and cents, and Tim Hortons was one of the most successful food-service businesses in Canada.

In truth, the achievements of Tim Hortons resonate with anyone who has spent time in Canada. It is impossible not to be aware of the prominence of the company's restaurants across the cities, towns and villages dotting the highways that criss-cross this country. But more than that, I feel Canadians respect Tim Hortons because they know it was developed in a way that integrated into the communities it served. It is a business first and foremost, of course, but it is an enterprise that customers, employees, store owners and communities can count on.

These days, Canadians visit Tim Hortons so regularly that they are often on a first-name basis with many of the employees of the restaurant they frequent. The average order is now between $2.50 and $2.80 per person, and 10 percent of all of the chain's customers visit a Tim Hortons more than ten times a week, while 40 percent visit up to four times a week. To say the chain has developed a loyal customer base would be underplaying the connection between Tim Hortons' customers and the restaurants.

While our competitors built their operations on selling franchises that were big on flash but had little substance, Tim Hortons was built upon a foundation of honest and straightforward business principles. Everything was "always fresh"—in terms of our way of thinking, our products and the way we presented the stores. The chain always aimed at being head and shoulders above our competition. Since many of the original competitors of Tim Hortons have long since disappeared, it is clear which business strategy has prevailed.

Though some people may recognize my role in the Tim Hortons plot, it was not a story I wrote on my own. There's no business in the world that became a success entirely on the work of a single individual. In that respect, Tim Hortons is not any different. In truth, TDL and Tim Hortons were made successful through the hard work and dedication of thousands of people over the course of forty years. Those individuals, who are too numerous to name, worked countless hours away from their friends and families to make Tim Hortons the most successful and largest domestic food-service company Canada has ever been witness to. These people deserve to be applauded and recognized for their efforts.

Certainly, the chain has changed over the past few years. The Tim Hortons that rose in the 1960s has long since been replaced by modern restaurants. Several of the original stores in places like Hamilton have been closed or moved to more desirable locations. Some of the best stores from the early years of the business have seen their signs taken down and their buildings converted to pharmacies and other businesses. While the chain has pushed forward with newer stores, the history of Tim Hortons can still be seen in Hamilton. It was Tim's dream to make the restaurant that used his name a success, and today, four decades after it opened on May 17, 1964, the first store still stands in its original location.

Some things have changed at that first store since I first walked through the front door in 1965 to learn the art of preparing a donut. The store underwent a full renovation several years ago, and today has more space and parking than the original. To reflect the role of the restaurant in the city's history, the stretch of Ottawa Street near Dunsmuir now bears the honourary designation of "Tim Hortons Way." But the restaurant still rests on the same busy street corner, a testament to the resiliency and vibrancy of Tim Hortons. I only wish Tim had had the opportunity to see the great things the restaurant chain that was named after him has accomplished.

Sometimes, great things can be accomplished in the shadow of tragedy. As a celebration of Tim's life, the Tim Horton Memorial Camp was created. From that emerged the Tim Horton Children's Foundation and its six camps that stretch across Canada and even into the U.S. These camps have provided a ray of hope for kids who have struggled in a difficult world. Thousands of children attend the camps each year, and I'm sure Tim would be proud that this noble effort uses his name.

Was selling TDL and the Tim Hortons brand a mistake? I don't think there is any question that it was. If I were to do it again, the situation would have been handled very differently. Instead of trying to find the right partner to merge with, I would have pursued taking Tim Hortons onto the public markets, just as Wendy's was forced to do. In Canada, there's a remarkable amount of interest in the company, and I'm sure if we had taken TDL public in 1995, thousands of Canadians would have been delighted to own a piece of the chain.

As for me, I've thoroughly enjoyed my life away from Tim Hortons. If I had it to do all over again—if I could take a mulligan, as it were—I would never sell my baby, but the money I received from the sale has allowed me to follow my dreams and my passions. It allowed me to live a life I never could have imagined as a child growing up in Tatamagouche—or as an adult working multiple jobs just to get by in Hamilton. Thanks to my success, I have *Destination Fox Harb'r*, which has sailed more than 35,000 nautical miles; I've used it to bring friends and family along to witness some of the most spectacular and wonderful places on this earth.

The money I earned through Tim Hortons has also allowed me to give back to Canada in a variety of ways, including donating to educational and medical institutions, as well as providing significantly for the Children's Camps. As much as the Tim Hortons chain, the Children's Foundation is my legacy.

Given its inauspicious beginnings, it is remarkable to consider how Tim Hortons has become part of the fabric of Canadian life. Though the chain's popularity is now unparalleled, with nearly 3,000 restaurants in the chain, Tim Hortons has long been a place of importance to the people who live here.

More than thirty years ago, I recall getting in my car on a wonderful Saturday evening and driving down the highway from Hamilton to Brantford, where our new store had opened on Colborne Street. Though I arrived as the sun began to set, the parking lot of the new restaurant was full of life. I sat parked in my car and watched people come and go from the store. Many had their children with them, and they went in for beverages and donuts. They came out with smiles on their faces. These were people who perhaps did not have a lot of money, but took their kids out for a treat by taking them to Tims. It was amazing, just sitting and watching these people enter and leave the restaurant. It was one of the first opportunities in which I just observed how much enjoyment people received from Tim Hortons.

Though it was a long way from the giant chain it would become, I knew then that we had a company that connected with people. Tim Hortons registered with its customers in a way that is truly rare in business.

Tim Hortons restaurants have become meeting places for people and communities across this country. In many ways, these restaurants, which began in such humble circumstances, have become the hub of Canada. It has been a remarkable experience to play a role in its development, and I'm just pleased to have been a witness to it along the way.

APPENDIX A

We've only just begun...

Dear Friends and Colleagues:

It is with a great deal of pride that we now share in the celebration of the Tim Horton chain's silver anniversary. Twenty-five years ago, Store #1 opened in Hamilton, Ontario. A converted service station with 1,200 sq. ft. of space brought annual sales of $50,000. This store is now owned by Dave and Maureen Sauve and I think it's safe to say that sales have increased since year one! In fact, in its silver anniversary, sales are up 20% over last year.

Since the first store opening in 1964, the Tim Horton system has grown to Canada's only national and largest donut chain. What a tremendous success story — store owners, managers, staff, suppliers and a very loyal clientele working as a team from coast to coast.

While the appearance of our stores may have changed over the years, the basic guidelines of our operation have remained constant. Our guiding principles still focus on quality, cleanliness, service and price value. Tim Hortons has responded to the demands of a changing consumer society without compromising these principles.

The competitive pressures have changed and increased significantly over our twenty-five years of operation. We no longer compete only with donut shops in a limited sphere, but must now fend off the aggressive strategies of convenience stores, supermarkets and assorted food chains who are diversifying to include many of our core products.

No longer merely a donut shop, our marketing directives and objectives run through several planes, leaving us in a unique category of our own. We no longer have to be limited by the term donuts in our signage, but instead look to the universal popularity and all-encompassing name of Tim Hortons alone to lead us into the next twenty-five years on a strong and committed course.

Some of our stores now occupy over 3,000 sq. ft. of space with seating capacities in excess of 100. Our product mix is monitored constantly to keep abreast of consumer trends and preferences. Coffee, muffins and cookies have had the greatest sales increases on average in our stores, while soups, sandwiches, chili and bagels are recent menu additions showing strong potential. We are continually testing new and varied products that will keep us on the leading edge of the marketplace.

There are now more than 420 stores presently operating within the Tim Horton system, with thirty of these stores enjoying sales in excess of one million dollars. Two of these stores are rapidly approaching two million dollars in sales. By year end we should reach 450 stores with total system-wide sales of 275 million dollars.

Our plan is to increase our system by a minimum of fifty new stores per year, with an additional fifty existing stores being rebuilt, renovated or upgraded annually. Varied store locations have created new opportunities for us, such as sites on highways, in universities, hospitals, business parks and major tourist attractions.

Our continuing success is the result of many factors: our good fortune in attracting outstanding and committed store owners; our strong and reliable group of suppliers which has enabled us to develop a consistently high calibre of products in sync with consumer trends; our store location and decors, which offer a comfortable atmosphere to our customers; our success in finding and developing excellent people to manage our part of the franchisor/franchisee partnership in Tim Donut Limited.

Our efforts within the community through the Tim Horton Children's Foundation have been a rewarding experience for all involved. The dedication of our store owners and staff who have helped to make our camp facilities a reality has been most gratifying. The Tatamagouche and Parry Sound camps provided "a holiday to remember" for some 1,200 children again this past summer. A new 10,000 sq. ft. main lodge is also under construction at the Parry Sound camp and is expected to be ready to welcome campers in June, 1990. We are delighted to announce that, pending the signing of formal documents, construction will soon begin on the Tim Horton ranch in Kananaskis Country, Alberta. We are actively pursuing a Quebec location for the fourth camp. Ideally this location should be near Ottawa so our children have the opportunity of visiting our nation's capital with its impressive parliament buildings and its tremendous historic and educational sites.

We look back with pride on twenty-five years of operation, service and growth. The efforts and contributions of each of the store owners, managers and staff, all of our suppliers and our Tim Donut Limited management and staff are clearly reflected in the success we have enjoyed. May I add my personal thanks to each and every one of you, and express my confidence in your abilities to take us enthusiastically and successfully into our next twenty-five years of business. I believe the success story for the Tim Horton chain has only just begun.

Kindest regards,

Ronald V. Joyce,
C.E.O.

A letter I sent out to friends and colleagues after 25 years in operation.

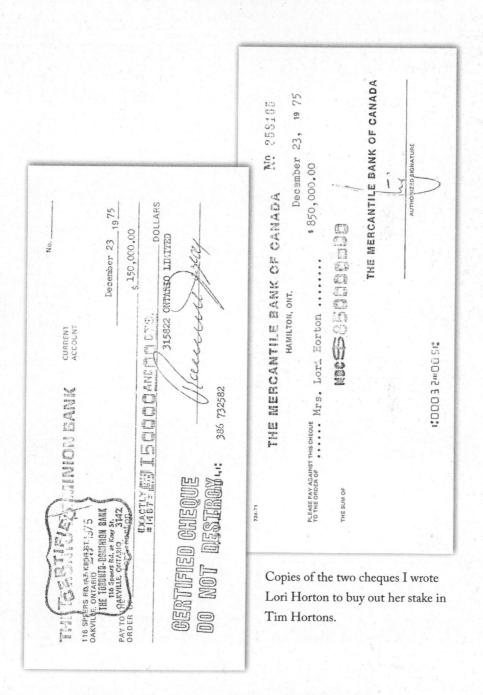

Copies of the two cheques I wrote
Lori Horton to buy out her stake in
Tim Hortons.

T I M   H O R T O N   D O N U T .

FORMULAS   & R ECIPIES.

FRANCHISE OPERATOR :   ....

(TO BE HELD IN STICT CONFIDENCE.)

The original Tim Hortons manual given to Spencer Brown when he purchased the first Tim Hortons. He gave the manual to me several years after I had purchased the store.

" Yeast Raised Donuts"

1. Make sure the dough is well developed, approximately three minutes after clean-up.

2. Scale all ingredients carefully particularly with regards to the water. not guess but scale.

3. Dough temperature from mixer should be 80 to 82° F. A few degrees variation either up or down will change the time of fermentation.

4. Give dough approxmately ##/####### 45 to 50 minutes fermentation, then cut into heads and mold these to expel all gases.

5. Approximately 20 min. rest time before pinning out. Make sure dough heads are sufficiently relaxed to work freely under the pin.

6. Pin out evenly and relax the dough well before cutting.

7. Proof with just enough moisture to keep donuts from crusting heavily.

8. Donuts should be dry before going to fryer.

9. Give good three quarter proofing. Under proofing is one reason for donuts blowing in the fat.

10. Large air holes in the finished donut is an indication that the dough was not sufficiently relaxed before pinning out, and all the old gases were not expelled during molding of the dough heads.

11. When scrap dough is added to a new batch watch fermentation carefully. The addition of very much scrap will hasten this fermentation period. Due to the fact that the yeast in the scrap has attained a high grow th rate. If the amount of scrap added is very high, it will benecessary to cut slightly on the yeast content in the new dough, or take the dough sooner.

12. Frying at proper temperature is very important. it should take approxmately 90 seconds.

13. Too low a temperature will increase this time, thereby increasing absorbtion and decreasing shelf life.

14. Too high a temperature will seal and colour the outside of the donut too quickly and product will be doughy inside also will lack full volume.

15. Proper temperature is from 375 to 385 ° F.

Tim HORTON DONUT FORMULA'S

White Cake Donut

10 lb. cold water
30 lb. # 7 cake mix
Mix 1 min. in first, 2 min. in second.

Same for choc cake

Smaller batches use ratio of water
to mix 1/3

Yeast donut Formula

Mix.
    15 lb. warm water

    30 lb. Fridoe mix

    13/4 lb. Yeast.

    1 Capfull vanilla.

Mix in ~~yeast~~ first until well mixed together

Mix in second for 15 min.

in the third untill dough is pulled away from side of bowl.

FRENCH CRULLER

    5 lb. mix.

    Add water until mixed until fluffy.

    2 qts. of eggs added 1/2 at a time ,

    mix everything together until well mixed.

GLAZE

15 lb. water

3 lb. Glucose

60 lb. Icing sugar

3 oz. Geletin

Mix in 1 qt. of hot water to be added after above well mixed
mix in first gear until mixed.

CHOC. ICING

4 lb. choc. fondant

4 lb. Van. fondant

50 lb. Icing sugar

10 lb. Wa ter.

   Add water as mixing for consistency, mix in first
until ingredients mixed, in second 5 min., in third until
well mixed, 1 min. in high.

MAPLE ICING

6 lb. Maple Fudge

3 lb. Glucose

40 lb. icing sugar

10 lb. cold Water

Add to mix same as choc.

APPENDIX D

Gordon Teter 8/2/95
Ron Deal 8/7/95

SHARES   16,200

EXCLUDED ASSETS   FLOAT PLANE
                         EXCAVATOR
                         CITATION

PURCHASE OPTION @ NBV   BEANSVILLE (MAR 87
                         MAINWAY   -84)

BEST EFFORTS TO GET CAMPBELLVILLE
HOUSE TO FOUNDATION BEFORE
OR AFTER CLOSING OR VERY FAVORABLE
LEASE WHICH WOULDN'T FORCE
ASSET WRITE-OFF

RVT NTE $12 SHR WITH ADJ FOR
CAMPBELLVILLE DONATION IF NECESSARY

CLOSING NOT BEFORE DEC 29
NOR LATER THAN JAN 2 AT
WII OPTION

WENDY'S BOARD SEAT & COMPENSATION
PACKAGE AS OUTLINED IN LETTER

After weeks of negotiating details, Gord Teter and I drafted the rough deal out on
a piece of paper using a red marker in the washroom of a Burlington convention
centre. Less than a week later the news would be made public that I had sold TDL
to Wendy's.

ACKNOWLEDGEMENTS

The process of writing a book is certainly challenging and time consuming, and throughout the creation of *Always Fresh*, several friends and associates helped in its development, including Robert Thompson, who put countless hours into the writing, the Honourable Ed Lumley, Buck Bennet, my mentor and friend, and his wife Lois, my assistant Andrea Rosgen, the Honourable Michael Harris, Arch Jollymore, Gary O'Neill and his wife Mary, Paul Bates, Tim Armstrong, Dave Sobey, Vi Twamley, Larissa Barranco, Debi Mattatall, Louise Good and Lynn McKay. Also, my former assistant and dear friend, Michele Thornley, gave generously of her time in helping recall key instances in the history of Tim Hortons, as did Dave Keon, Debbie Burch and Craig St. Germain.

I'd also like to thank my editor at HarperCollins, Jim Gifford, who oversaw the development of the book, as well as copyeditor Lloyd Davis, who helped refine the content. Similarly, I need to recognize the contributions of Hilary McMahon of Westwood Creative in getting this project off the ground.

I'd like to personally thank every one of the kind and generous individuals who selflessly gave their time to the Tim Horton Children's Foundation over the past three decades. There are numerous Tim Hortons pioneers who invested their time in helping found, create and foster the Tim Horton Memorial Camp and later the Tim Horton Children's Camps across Canada and in the U.S.

In particular I'd like to thank some of the earliest franchise owners, like my good friend Layton Coulter, Jim Gillies and his sister Laurie, John and Carol Hoey, Charlie Hughes, Steve Kennish, Joe Lapsevich, Reid and Joanne Manore, Ed and Florence Mattatall, George and Dorothy McGlinchey, Pat and Pat McGrinder, John and Cora Miszuk, Danny Murphy, Don and Sharon Pritlove, Jim Rushak, George and Elizabeth Shaw, Alec and Wilma Strom, Jim and Joyce Tennants, and Gary and Karen Wilson and George Rumble, who were key in helping promote and develop the Children's Camp vision that has come to help so many children. I also thank my good friend Ken Gerrie of Gerrie Electric who donated many electrical supplies and gave us favourable pricing for other materials for the camp, Garland Industries and Diversey for donating our kitchen equipment, the Oakville Rod & Gun Club and Brian Chamberlain and Associates for the architectural drawings of many of the camps. Similarly, Ed Marshall and his wife Lois were central in helping found the camp in Kannaskis country in Alberta. Also, my former assistant of many years, Elisabeth Fayt, was very dedicated to the foundation. Dale Jollymore deserves special thanks for generously donating his time in finding volunteers to help construct the camps across Canada.

Some who dedicated their time are no longer with us, but their contribution to the Children's Camps should be acknowledged, including my brother Willard, Carl Stewart, Bud Kennish, Bill Hunter, Doug Christie, as well as Justice Dick Trainor.

I'd also like to thank my sister Gwen Oliver and her husband Gord for helping me raise the money to buy the second store in Hamilton. Similarly, I'd also like to thank Alan Pyle, who believed in the Tim Hortons concept and helped finance it along the way.

Finally, I'd like to acknowledge every current and former Tim Hortons employee, past and present store owners, as well as the millions and millions of Canadians who regularly stopped by over the past 40-plus years. Thank you all for helping make my dream such a success.

—Ron Joyce

ooooo

I would like to thank Ron Joyce for allowing me to see the inner workings of an amazing man and a great company. Lots of black Tim Hortons coffee was consumed along the way and it has been quite the adventure.

I'd also like to thank Hilary McMahon for helping develop the project, Jim Gifford for believing in it, and Andrea Rosgen for working so tirelessly throughout the process. I'd also like to recognize the help of Larissa Barranco, Tim Armstrong and all the other people who work with Ron and provided assistance at some point with this book. I'd also like to especially recognize the time and efforts of a Tim Hortons pioneer, Gary O'Neill, who helped on several key instances as this book came to life.

Thanks also to the management of the *National Post* for agreeing to give me the time off to work on *Always Fresh*.

Several of my closest friends, like Ben Cowan-Dewar, Ian Andrew and Steve Waxman, also provided great support over the months the book was written.

Lastly, thanks to Jennifer, my beautiful wife, and my stunning daughter Sydney, for giving me the time and energy to take on such a big and important project.

—Robert Thompson

INDEX